Clean Python

Elegant Coding in Python

Sunil Kapil

Apress®

Clean Python: Elegant Coding in Python

Sunil Kapil
Sunnyvale, CA, USA

ISBN-13 (pbk): 978-1-4842-4877-5   ISBN-13 (electronic): 978-1-4842-4878-2
https://doi.org/10.1007/978-1-4842-4878-2

Copyright © 2019 by Sunil Kapil

Managing Director, Apress Media LLC: Welmoed Spahr
Acquisitions Editor: Nikhil Karkal
Development Editor: Rita Fernando
Coordinating Editor: Divya Modi

Cover designed by eStudioCalamar

Cover image designed by Freepik (www.freepik.com)

Distributed to the book trade worldwide by Springer Science+Business Media New York, 233 Spring Street, 6th Floor, New York, NY 10013. Phone 1-800-SPRINGER, fax (201) 348-4505, e-mail orders-ny@springer-sbm.com, or visit www.springeronline.com. Apress Media, LLC is a California LLC and the sole member (owner) is Springer Science + Business Media Finance Inc (SSBM Finance Inc). SSBM Finance Inc is a **Delaware** corporation.

For information on translations, please e-mail rights@apress.com, or visit www.apress.com/rights-permissions.

Apress titles may be purchased in bulk for academic, corporate, or promotional use. eBook versions and licenses are also available for most titles. For more information, reference our Print and eBook Bulk Sales web page at www.apress.com/bulk-sales.

Any source code or other supplementary material referenced by the author in this book is available to readers on GitHub via the book's product page, located at www.apress.com/9781484248775. For more detailed information, please visit www.apress.com/source-code.

Printed on acid-free paper

Table of Contents

About the Author

Sunil Kapil has been in the software profession for the past ten years, writing production code in Python and several other languages. He has worked as a software engineer primarily on the backend for web and mobile services. He has developed, deployed, and maintained small to large projects in production that are being loved and used by millions of users. He has completed these projects with small to large teams in different professional environments for well-known software companies around the world. He is also a passionate advocate of open source and continuously contributes to projects such as Zulip Chat and Black. Additionally, he works with nonprofit organizations and contributes to their software projects on a volunteer basis.

Sunil is a frequent speaker at various meetups and conferences and has given frequent talks about Python.

You can visit his web site about software engineering, tools, and techniques. On top of that, you can reach out to him by e-mail or follow him on social media.

Web: https://softwareautotools.com/
E-mail: snlkapil@gmail.com
Twitter: @snlkapil (https://twitter.com/snlkapil)
LinkedIn: https://www.linkedin.com/in/snlkapil/
GitHub: https://github.com/skapil

About the Technical Reviewer

Sonal Raj (@_sonalraj) has been an author, engineer, mentor, and avid Pythonista for more than 10 years. He is a Goldman Sachs alumnus and a former research fellow at the Indian Institute of Science. He is an integral part of the financial technology industry with expertise in building trading algorithms and low latency systems. He is an open source developer and community member.

Sonal has master's degrees in information technology and business administration. His domains of research include distributed systems, graph databases, and education technology. He is an active member of the Institution of Engineering and Technology (IET), London, and a lifetime member of the Indian Society for Technical Education.

He is the author of the book *Neo4j High Performance,* about the functioning and use of the graph database Neo4j. He is also the author of the Interview Essentials series of books focusing on technical interview methodologies. Sonal is also an editor at People Chronicles Media, a reviewer for the *Journal of Open Source Software* (JOSS), and a founder of the Yugen Foundation.

Acknowledgments

First, I would like to thank Nikhil of Apress. Nikhil contacted me in October 2018 and persuaded me to write a book with Apress Media LLC. Next, I would like to thank Divya Modi, coordinating editor at Apress, for her great support while writing the chapters and her great patience during my busy schedule. In addition, many thanks to Rita Fernando, development editor at Apress, who provided valuable suggestions during the review process that made the book more valuable for Python developers. Next, I would like to thank Sonal Raj for critically examining every single chapter. You found many issues that I would never have found.

Of course, I would like to say a big thank-you to the whole production team at Apress for supporting me.

Last but not least, I would like to thank my beloved and unique family, especially for their understanding that a book project takes a great deal of time. Thanks to my mother, Leela Kapil, and father, Harish Chandra Kapil, for all the encouragement and support.

My beloved wife Neetu: I deeply appreciate all your encouragement and support while writing this book; it has made all the difference. You are awesome!

Introduction

Python is one of the most popular languages today. Relatively new
fields such as data science, AI, robotics, and data analytics, along with
traditional professions such as web development and scientific research,
are embracing Python. It's increasingly important for programmers writing
code in a dynamic language like Python to make sure that the code is high-
quality and error-free. As a Python developer, you want to make sure that
the software you are building makes your users happy without going over
budget or never releasing.

Python is a simple language, yet it's difficult to write great code because
there aren't many resources that teach how to write better Python code.

Currently lacking in the Python world are code consistency, patterns,
and an understanding of good Pythonic code among developers. For every
Python programmer, great Pythonic code has a different meaning. The
reason for this could be that Python is being used in so many areas that it's
difficult to reach consensus among developers about specific patterns. In
addition, Python doesn't have any books about clean code like Java and
Ruby do. There have been attempts to write those kinds of books to bring
clarity to good Python practices, but those attempts have been few and far
between, and quickly frankly, they haven't been high-quality.

The main goal of this book is to provide tips to Python developers of
various levels so they can write better Python software and programs. This
book gives you various techniques irrespective of the field you use Python
in. This book covers all levels of Python, from basic to advanced, and
shows you how to make your code more Pythonic.

Remember, writing software is not only science but art, and this book
will teach you how to become a better Python programmer.

CHAPTER 1

Pythonic Thinking

The thing that sets Python apart from other languages is that it is a simple language with a lot of depth. Because it's simple, it's much more important to write code cautiously, especially in a big project, because it's easy for the code to become complex and bloated. Python has a philosophy called the Zen of Python, which emphasizes simplicity over complexity.[1]

In this chapter, you will learn about some common practices that can help you to make your Python code more readable and simpler. I will cover some well-known practices, as well as some that might not be so well-known. While writing your next project or working on your current project, make sure that you are well aware of these Python practices so you can improve your code.

Note In the Python world, following the Zen of Python philosophy makes your code "Pythonic." There are lots of good practices that have been recommended in the Python official documentation to make your code cleaner and more readable. Reading the PEP8 guide will surely help you to understand why some practices are recommended.

---

[1]https://www.python.org/dev/peps/pep-0020/

© Sunil Kapil 2019

S. Kapil, *Clean Python*, https://doi.org/10.1007/978-1-4842-4878-2_1

Write Pythonic Code

Python has some official documentation called PEP8 that defines best practices for writing Pythonic code. This style guide has evolved over time. You can check it out at `https://www.python.org/dev/peps/pep-0008/`.

In this chapter, you will focus on some common practices defined in PEP8 and see how following those rules can benefit you as a developer.

Naming

As a developer, I have worked with different languages such as Java, NodeJS, Perl, and Golang. All these languages have naming conventions for variables, functions, classes, and so on. Python also recommends using naming conventions. I will discuss some of the naming conventions in this section that you should follow while writing Python code.

Variables and Functions

You should name functions and variables in lowercase with the words separated by underscores, as this will improve readability. See Listing 1-1.

Listing 1-1. Variable Names

```
names = "Python"                        # variable name
job_title = "Software Engineer"         # variable name
                                        with underscore

populated_countries_list = []           # variable name
                                        with underscore
```

You should also consider using nonmangling method names in your code and using one underscore (_) or two underscores (__). See Listing 1-2.

Listing 1-2. Nonmangling Names

```
_books = {}                    # variable name to define
                               private
__dict = []                    # prevent name mangling with
                               python in-build lib
```

You should use one underscore (_) as a prefix for the internal variable of a class, where you don't want an outside class to access the variable. This is just a convention; Python doesn't make a variable with a single underscore prefix private.

Python has a convention for functions as well, as shown in Listing 1-3.

Listing 1-3. Normal Function Names

```
# function name with single underscore
def get_data():
    ---
    ---

def calculate_tax_data():
    ----
```

The same rules apply to private methods and methods where you want to prevent name mangling with built-in Python functions. See Listing 1-4.

Listing 1-4. Function Names to Represent Private Methods and Nonmangling

```
# Private method with single underscore
def _get_data():
    ---
    ---
```

```
# double underscore to prevent name mangling with other
in-build functions
def __path():
    ----
    ----
```

In addition to following these naming rules, it's important to use specific names instead of having obscure names for your functions or variables.

Let's consider a function that returns a user object when provided with a user ID. See Listing 1-5.

Listing 1-5. Function Names

```
# Wrong Way
def get_user_info(id):
    db = get_db_connection()
    user = execute_query_for_user(id)
    return user

# Right way
def get_user_by(user_id):
    db = get_db_connection()
    user = execute_user_query(user_id)
    return user
```

Here, the second function, get_user_by, makes sure you are using the same vocabulary for passing a variable, which gives the right context for the function. The first function, get_user_info, is ambiguous because the parameter id could mean anything. Is it a user table index ID or a user payment ID or any other ID? This kind of code can create confusion for other developers using your API. To fix this, I changed two things in the second function; I changed the function name and passed an argument name, which makes code much more readable. When reading the second function, you know right away the purpose of the function and expected value from the function.

As a developer, it's your responsibility to think carefully while naming your variables and functions to make the code readable for other developers.

Classes

The name of classes should be in camel case like in most other languages. Listing 1-6 shows a simple example.

Listing 1-6. Class Names

```
class UserInformation:
    def get_user(id):
        db = get_db_connection()
        user = execute_query_for_user(id)
        return user
```

Constants

You should define constant names with capital letters. Listing 1-7 shows an example.

Listing 1-7. Constant Names

```
TOTAL = 56
TIMOUT = 6
MAX_OVERFLOW = 7
```

Function and Method Arguments

Function and method arguments should follow the same rules as variables and method names. A class method has self as the first keyword argument compared to functions that don't pass self as a keyword parameter. See Listing 1-8.

Listing 1-8. Function and Method Arguments

```
def calculate_tax(amount, yearly_tax):
    ----


class Player:
    def get_total_score(self, player_name):
        ----
```

Expressions and Statements in Your Code

At some point you might have tried to write code in a clever way to save some lines or impress your colleagues. However, there are costs to writing clever code: readability and simplicity. Let's take a look at the piece of code in Listing 1-9, which sorts a nested dictionary.

Listing 1-9. Sort a Nested Dictionary

```
users = [{"first_name":"Helen", "age":39},
        {"first_name":"Buck", "age":10},
        {"first_name":"anni", "age":9}
        ]
users = sorted(users, key=lambda user: user["first_name"].
lower())
```

What's the problem with this code?

Well, you are sorting this nested dictionary by first_name using a lambda in one line, which makes it looks like a clever way to sort the dictionary instead of using a loop.

However, it's not easy to understand this code at first glance, especially for new developers, because lambdas are not an easy concept to grasp because of their quirky syntax. Of course, you are saving lines here by using a lambda because it allows you to sort the dictionary in clever way;

however, this doesn't make this code correct or readable. This code fails to address issues such as missing keys or if the dictionary is correct or not.

Let's rewrite this code using a function and try to make the code more readable and correct; the function will check for all unexpected values and is much simpler to write. See Listing 1-10.

Listing 1-10. Sorted Dictionary by Function

```python
users = [{"first_name":"Helen", "age":39},
        {"first_name":"Buck", "age":10},
        {"name":"anni", "age":9}
        ]

def get_user_name(users):
"""Get name of the user in lower case"""
    return users["first_name"].lower()

def get_sorted_dictionary(users):
"""Sort the nested dictionary"""
if not isinstance(users, dict):
    raise ValueError("Not a correct dictionary")
if not len(users):
    raise ValueError("Empty dictionary")

users_by_name = sorted(users, key=get_user_name)
return users_by_name
```

As you can see, this code checks for all possible unexpected values, and it's much more readable than the previous one-line code. One-line code saves you lines but injects a lot of complexity into your code. That doesn't necessarily mean that one-line code is bad; the point I am trying to make here is that if your one-line code makes it harder to read the code, please avoid it.

You have to make those decisions consciously while writing code. Sometimes writing one-line code makes your code readable, and sometimes not.

Let's consider one more example, where you are trying to read a CSV file and count the number of lines processed by the CSV file. The code in Listing 1-11 shows you why it's important to make your code readable and how naming plays a big role in making your code readable.

Breaking code into helper function helps to make complex code readable and easy to debug when you hit a specific error in your production code.

Listing 1-11. Reading a CSV File

```python
import csv

with open("employee.csv", mode="r") as csv_file:
    csv_reader = csv.DictReader(csv_file)
    line_count = 0
    for row in csv_reader:
        if line_count == 0:
            print(f'Column names are {", ".join(row)}')
            line_count += 1
            print(f'\t{row["name"]} salary: {row["salary"]}'
                    f'and was born in {row["birthday month"]}.')
        line_count += 1
    print(f'Processed {line_count} lines.')
```

Here the code is doing multiple things in the with statement. To make it more readable, you can pull out the code with process salary from the CSV file into a different function to make it less error prone. It's difficult to debug this kind of code when lots of things are going on in a few lines, so you'll want to make sure that you have clear goals and boundaries when defining your function. So, let's break it down little further in Listing 1-12.

Listing 1-12. Reading a CSV File, with More Readable Code

```python
import csv

with open('employee.txt', mode='r') as csv_file:
    csv_reader = csv.DictReader(csv_file)
    line_count = 0
    process_salary(csv_reader)

def process_salary(csv_reader):
"""Process salary of user from csv file."""
    for row in csv_reader:
        if line_count == 0:
            print(f'Column names are {", ".join(row)}')
            line_count += 1
        print(f'\t{row["name"]} salary: {row["salary"]}')
        line_count += 1
    print(f'Completed {line_count} lines.')
```

Here you created a helper function instead of writing everything in the with statement. This makes it clear to the reader what actually the process_salary function does. If you want to handle a specific exception or want to read more data from a CSV file, you can further break down this function to follow the single responsibility principle.

Embrace the Pythonic Way to Write Code

PEP8 has some recommendations to follow when you write your code that will make your Python code much cleaner and more readable. Let's look some of those practices.

Prefer join Instead of In-Place String Concatenation

Wherever you are concerned about performance in your code, use the "".
join() method instead of in-place string concatenation, as in a += b or
a = a + b. The "".join() method guarantees leaner time concatenation
across various Python implementations.

The reason for this is that when you use join, Python allocates
memory for the joined string only one time, but when you concatenate
strings, Python has to allocate new memory for each concatenation
because the Python string is immutable. See Listing 1-13.

Listing 1-13. Using the join Method

```python
first_name = "Json"
last_name = "smart"

# Not a recommended way to concatenate string
full_name = first_name + "  " +  last_name

# More performant and improve readability
" ".join([first_name, last_name])
```

Consider Using is and is not Whenever You Need to Compare with None

Always use is or is not for comparison with None. Keep this in mind while
writing code such as the following:

```python
if val:                  # Will work when val is not None
```

Make sure to keep in mind that you are considering val to be None and
not some other container type such as dict or set. Let's look further to
understand where this kind of code can surprise you.

In the previous line of code, val is an empty dictionary; however, val is considered false, which might not want in your code, so be careful while writing this kind of code.

Don't do this:

```
val = {}
if val:                    # This will be false in python context
```

Instead, write code as explicit as possible to make your code less error prone.

Do this:

```
if val is not None:       # Make sure only None value will be false
```

Prefer Using is not Instead of not ... is

There is no difference between using is not and using not ... is. However, the is not syntax is more readable compared to not ... is.

Don't do this:

```
if not val is None:
```

Do this:

```
if val is not None:
```

Consider Using a Function Instead of a Lambda When Binding to an Identifier

When you are assigning a lambda expression to a specific identifier, consider using a function. lambda is a keyword in Python to perform one-line operations; however, using lambda for writing a function might not be as good a choice as writing a function using def.

Don't do this:

```
square = lambda x: x * x
```

Do this:

```
def square(val):
    return val * val
```

The def square(val) function object is more useful for string representation and traceback than the generic <lambda>. This kind of use eliminates the usefulness of lambdas. Consider using lambdas in larger expressions so you don't impact the readability of code.

Be Consistent with the return Statement

If the function is expected to return a value, make sure all the execution paths of that function return the value. It's good practice to make sure you have a return expression in all the places your function exits. But if a function is expected to simply perform an action without returning a value, Python implicitly returns None as the default from the function.

Don't do this:

```
def calculate_interest(principle, time rate):
    if principle > 0:
        return (principle * time * rate) / 100

def calculate_interest(principle, time rate):
    if principle < 0:
        return
    return (principle * time * rate) / 100
```

Do this:

```
def calculate_interest(principle, time rate):
    if principle > 0:
        return (principle * time * rate) / 100
    else:
        return None

def calculate_interest(principle, time rate):
    if principle < 0:
        return None
    return (principle * time * rate) / 100
```

Prefer Using "".startswith() and "".endswith()

When you need to check prefixes or suffixes, consider using "". startswith() and "".endswith() instead of slicing. slice is a really useful method for slicing a string, but might get better performance when you are slicing a big string or performing string operations. However, if you are doing something as simple as checking for a prefix or suffix, go for either startswith or endswith because it makes it obvious to the reader that you are checking for a prefix or suffix in a string. In other words, it makes your code more readable and cleaner.

Don't do this:

```
Data = "Hello, how are you doing?"
if data.startswith("Hello")
```

Do this:

```
data = "Hello, how are you doing?"
if data[:5] == "Hello":
```

Use the isinstance() Method Instead of type() for Comparison

When you are comparing two objects' types, consider using isinstance() instead of type because isinstance() is true for subclasses. Consider a scenario where you are passing a data structure that is the subclass of a dict like orderdict. type() will fail for that specific type of data structure; however, isinstance() will recognize that it's the subclass of dict.

Don't do this:

```
user_ages = {"Larry": 35, "Jon": 89, "Imli": 12}
type(user_ages) == dict:
```

Do this:

```
user_ages = {"Larry": 35, "Jon": 89, "Imli": 12}
if isinstance(user_ages, dict):
```

Pythonic Way to Compare Boolean Values

There are multiple ways to compare Boolean values in Python.

Don't do this:

```
if is_empty = False
if is_empty == False:
if is_empty is False:
```

Do this:

```
is_empty = False
if is_empty:
```

Write Explicit Code for Context Manager

When you are writing code in the with statement, consider using a function to do any operation that's different from acquire and release.

Don't do this:

```python
class NewProtocol:
    def __init__(self, host, port, data):
        self.host = host
        self.port = port
        self.data = data

    def __enter__(self):
        self._client = Socket()
        self._client.connect((self.host,
                                    self.port))
        self._transfer_data(data)

    def __exit__(self, exception, value, traceback):
        self._receive_data()
        self._client.close()

    def _transfer_data(self):
        ---

    def _receive_data(self):
        ---

con = NewProtocol(host, port, data)
with con:
    transfer_data()
```

Do this:

```python
#connection
class NewProtocol:
    def __init__(self, host, port):
        self.host = host
        self.port = port
```

```
    def __enter__(self):
        self._client = socket()
        self._client.connect((self.host,
                                  self.port))

    def __exit__(self, exception, value, traceback):
        self._client.close()

    def transfer_data(self, payload):
        ...
    def receive_data(self):
        ...

with connection.NewProtocol(host, port):
    transfer_data()
```

In the second statement, the __enter__ and __exit__ methods of
Python are doing some stuff besides opening and closing the connection.
It's better to be explicit and write different functions to do the other
operations that aren't acquiring and closing the connection.

Use Linting Tools to Improve Python Code

Code linters are important tools to format your code consistently. Having a
consistent code format across a project is valuable.

Linting tools basically solve these problems for you:

- Syntax errors

- Structure such as unused variables or passing correct
  arguments to function

- Pointing out violations of the PEP8 guidelines

Linting tools make you much more productive as a developer because
they save you a lot of time by hunting down issues at runtime. There are
multiple linting tools available for Python. Some of the tools handle a

specific part of linting like the docstring style of code quality, and popular python liniting tools like flak8/pylint check for all PEP8 rules and tools like mypy check specifically for python typing.

Either you can integrate all of them in your code or you can use one that covers the standard checks to make sure you are following the PEP8 style guide. Most notable are among them are Flake8 and Pylint. Whatever tool you go for, make sure it adheres to the rules of PEP8.

There are a few features to look for in linting tools:

- PEP8 rules adherence

- Imports ordering

- Naming (Python naming convention for variables, functions, classed, modules, files, etc.)

- Circular imports

- Code complexity (check the complexity of function by looking number of lines, loops and other parameters)

- Spell-checker

- Docstring-style checks

There are different ways you can run linters.

- At programming time using an IDE

- At commit time using pre-commit tools

- At CI time by integrating with Jenkins, CircleCI, and so on

---

Note   These are some of the common practices that will definitely improve your code. If you want to take maximum advantage of Python good practices, please take a look at the PEP8 official documentation. Also, reading good code in GitHub will help you to understand how to write better Python code.

Using Docstrings

Docstrings are a powerful way to document your code in Python. Docstrings are usually written at the start of methods, classes, and modules. A docstring becomes the __doc__ special attribute of that object.

The Python official language recommends using """Triple double quotes""" to write docstrings. You can find these practices in the PEP8 official documentation. Let's briefly talk about some best practices for writing docstrings in your Python code. See Listing 1-14.

Listing 1-14. Function with a Docstring

```python
def get_prime_number():
    """Get list of prime numbers between 1 to 100."""
```

Python recommends a specific way to write docstrings. There are different ways to write docstrings, which we will discuss later in this chapter; however, all those different types follow some common rules. Python has defined the rules as follows:

- Triple quotes are used even if the string fits in one line. This practice is useful when you want to expand.

- There should not be any blank line before or after the string in triple quotes.

- Use a period (.) to end the statement in the docstring.

Similarly, Python multiline docstring rules can be applied to write multiline docstrings. Writing docstrings on multiple lines is one way to document your code in a bit more descriptive way. Instead of writing comments on every line, you can write descriptive docstrings in your Python code by leveraging Python multiline docstrings. This also helps other developers to find the documentation in the code itself instead of referring to documentation that is long and tiresome to read. See Listing 1-15.

Listing 1-15. Multiline Docstring

```
def call_weather_api(url, location):
"""Get the weather of specific location.

Calling weather api to check for weather by using weather api
and location. Make sure you provide city name only, country and
county names won't be accepted and will throw exception if not
found the city name.

:param url:  URL of the api to get weather.
:type url: str
:param location:  Location of the city to get the weather.
:type location: str
:return: Give the weather information of given location.
:rtype: str

"""
```

There are a few things to notice here.

- The first line is a brief description of the function or class.

- The end of the line has a period.

- There is a one-line gap between the brief description and the summary in docstrings.

You can write the same function if you are using Python 3 with the typing module, as shown in Listing 1-16.

Listing 1-16. Multiline Docstring with typing

```
def call_weather_api(url: str, location: str) -> str:
"""Get the weather of specific location.
```

Calling weather api to check for weather by using weather api and location. Make sure you provide city name only, country and county names won't be accepted and will throw exception if not found the city name.
```
"""
```

You don't need to write the parameter information if you are using the type in Python code.

As I've mentioned about different docstring types, new styles of docstrings have been introduced over the years by different sources. There is no better or recommended way to write a docstring. However, make sure you use the same style throughout the project for docstrings so they have consistent formatting.

There are four different ways to write a docstring.

- Here's a Google docstrings example:

```
"""Calling given url.
```

```
Parameters:
    url (str): url address to call.
```

```
Returns:
    dict: Response of the url api.
"""
```

- Here is a restructured text example (the official Python documents recommend this):

```
""" Calling given url.
```

```
:param url: Url to call.
:type url: str
```

```
:returns: Response of the url api.
:rtype: dict
"""
```

- Here is a NumPy/SciPy docstrings example:

```
""" Calling given url.

Parameters
----------
url : str
    URL to call.

Returns
-------
dict
    Response of url
"""
```

- Here's an Epytext example:

```
"""Call specific api.

@type url: str
@param file_loc: Call given url.
@rtype: dict
@returns: Response of the called api.
"""
```

Module-Level Docstrings

A module-level docstring should be put at the top of the file to describe the use of the module briefly. These comments should be before the import as well. A module docstring should focus on the goal of the module, including all the methods/classes in the module, instead of talking about a specific method or class. You can still specify a specific method or class briefly, if you think that the method or class has something that needs to be known at a high level by the client before using the module. See Listing 1-17.

Listing 1-17. Module Docstring

```
"""
This module contains all of the network related requests. This
module will check for all the exceptions while making the
network calls and raise exceptions for any unknown exception.
Make sure that when you use this module, you handle these
exceptions in client code as:
NetworkError exception for network calls.
NetworkNotFound exception if network not found.
"""

import urllib3
import json

....
```

You should consider doing the following when writing a docstring for a module:

- Write a brief description of the purpose of module.

- If you want to specify anything that could be useful for reader to know about module, like in Listing 1-15, you can add exception information, but take care not to go into too much detail.

- Consider the module docstring as a way to provide descriptive information about the module, without going into the detail of every function or class operation.

Make the Class Docstring Descriptive

The class docstring is mainly used to briefly describe the use of the class and its overall goal. Let's look at some examples to see how you can write class docstrings. See Listing 1-18.

Listing 1-18. Single-Line Docstring

```
class Student:
"""This class handle actions performed by a student."""

    def __init__(self):
        pass
```

This class has a one-line docstring, which briefly talks about the Student class. Make sure that you follow all the rules for one line, as described previously.

Let's consider the multiline docstring for a class that's shown in Listing 1-19.

Listing 1-19. Multiline Class Docstring

```
class Student:
    """Student class information.

    This class handle actions performed by a student.
    This class provides information about student full name,
    age, roll-number and other information.

    Usage:
    import student

    student = student.Student()
    student.get_name()
```

23

```
    >>> 678998
    """

  def __init__(self):
    pass
```

This class docstring is multiline; we wrote little more about the usage of Student class and how to use it.

Function Docstrings

Function docstrings can be written after a function or at the top of a function. Function docstrings mostly focus on describing the function's operation, and if you are not using Python typing, consider including parameters as well for See Listing 1-20 for example.

Listing 1-20. Function Docstring

```
def is_prime_number(number):
    """Check for prime number.

    Check the given number is prime number or not by checking
    against all the numbers less the square root of given number.

    :param number:  Given number to check for prime.
    :type number: int
    :return: True if number is prime otherwise False.
    :rtype: boolean
    """

        ...
```

Some Useful Docstring Tools

There are plenty of docstrings tools for Python. Docstring tools help to document the Python code by converting docstrings into HTML-formatted document files. These tools also help you update the document by running simple commands instead of manually maintaining the document. Making them part of your development flow makes them much more useful in the long run.

There are a few useful documentation tools. Every documentation tool has different goals, so which one you choose will depend upon your specific use case.

- *Sphinx*: http://www.sphinx-doc.org/en/stable/

  This is the most popular documentation tool for Python. This tool will autogenerate Python documents. It can generate multiple-format documentation files.

- *Pycco:* https://pycco-docs.github.io/pycco/

  This is quick way to generate documentation for your Python code. The main feature of this tool is to display code and documentation side-by-side.

- *Read the docs*: https://readthedocs.org/

  This is a popular tool in the open source community. Its main feature is to build, version, and host your docs for you.

- *Epydocs:* http://epydoc.sourceforge.net/

  This tool generates API documentation for Python modules based on their docstrings.

Using these tools will make it easier to maintain your code in the long run and will help you keep a consistent format for your code documentation.

Note   Docstrings are a great feature of Python and can make it really easy to document your code. Starting to use docstrings in your code as early as possible will make sure that you don't need to invest much time later when your project becomes much more mature with thousands of lines of code.

Write Pythonic Control Structures

Control structures are fundamental parts of any programming language, and it's true for Python as well. Python has a number of ways to write the control structure, but there are some best practices that will keep the Python code cleaner. We will look at these Python best practices for control structures in this section.

Use List Comprehensions

List comprehension is a way of writing code to solve an existing problem in a similar way as python for loop does however it allow to do that inside the list with or without if condition. There are multiple ways in Python to derive a list from another list. The main tools in Python for doing this are the `filter` and `map` methods. However, list comprehension is recommended way to do that as it makes your code much more readable compare to other options like map and filter.

In this example, you are trying to find the square of numbers with a map version:

```
numbers = [10, 45, 34, 89, 34, 23, 6]
square_numbers = map(lambda num: num**2, num)
```

Here is a list comprehension version:

```
square_numbers = [num**2 for num in numbers]
```

Let's look at another example where you use a filter for all true values. Here's the `filter` version:

```
data = [1, "A", 0, False, True]
filtered_data = filter(None, data)
```

Here is a list comprehension version:

```
filtered_data = [item for item in filter if item]
```

As you might have noticed, the list comprehension version is much more readable compared to the filter and map versions. The official Python documentation also recommends that you use list comprehension instead of `filter` and `map`.

If you don't have a complex condition or complex computation in the `for` loop, you should consider using list comprehension. But if you are doing many things in a loop, it's better to stick with a loop for readability purposes.

To further illustrate the point of using list comprehension over a `for` loop, let's look at an example where you need to identify a vowel from a list of characters.

```
list_char = ["a", "p", "t", "i", "y", "l"]
vowel = ["a", "e", "i", "o", "u"]
only_vowel = []
for item in list_char:
    if item in vowel:
        only_vowel.append(item)
```

Here's an example of using list comprehension:

```
[item for item in list_char if item in vowel]
```

As you can see, this example is much more readable when using list comprehension compared to using a loop but with fewer lines of code. Also, a loop has an extra performance cost because you need to append the item into the list each time, which you don't need to do in list comprehension.

Similarly, the `filter` and `map` functions have an extra cost to call the functions compared to list comprehension.

Don't Make Complex List Comprehension

You also want to make sure that the list comprehension is not too complex, which can hamper your code readability and make it prone to errors.

Let's consider another example of using list comprehension. List comprehension is good for at most two loops with one condition. Beyond that, it might start hampering the readability of the code.

Here's an example where you want to transpose this matrix:

```
matrix = [[1,2,3],
          [4,5,6],
          [7,8,9]]
```

and convert it to this one:

```
matrix = [[1,4,7],
          [2,5,8],
          [3,6,9]]
```

Using list comprehension, you might write it as follows:

```
return [[ matrix[row][col] for row in range(0, height) ] for
col in range(0,width) ]
```

Here the code is readable, and it makes sense to use list comprehension. You might even want to write the code in a better format such as the following:

```
return [[ matrix[row][col]
        for row in range(0, height) ]
        for col in range(0,width) ]
```

You can consider using loops instead of list comprehension when you have multiple if condition as follows:

```
ages = [1, 34, 5, 7, 3, 57, 356]
old = [age for age in ages if age > 10 and age < 100 and age is
not None]
```

Here, a lot of things are happening on one line, which is hard to read and error prone. It might be a good idea to use a for loop here instead of using list comprehension.

You can consider writing this code as follows:

```
ages = [1, 34, 5, 7, 3, 57, 356]
old = []
for age in ages:
    if age > 10 and age < 100:
        old.append(age)
print(old)
```

As you can see, this has more lines of code, but it's readable and cleaner.

So, a good rule of thumb is to start with list comprehension, and when expressions start getting complex or readability starts getting hampered, convert to using a loop.

Note   Using list comprehension wisely can improve your code; however, overuse of list comprehension can hamper the code's readability. So, refrain from using list comprehension when you are going for complex statements, which may be more than one condition or loop.

Should You Use a Lambda?

You can consider using a lambda where it helps in the expression instead of using it as a replacement of a function. Let's consider the example in Listing 1-21.

Listing 1-21. Using a Lambda Without Assigning

```
data = [[7], [3], [0], [8], [1], [4]]
def min_val(data):
"""Find minimum value from the data list."""
    return min(data, key=lambda x:len(x))
```

Here the code is using a lambda as a throwaway function to find a minimum value. However, I would advise you *not* to use a lambda as an anonymous function like this:

```
min_val = min(data, key=lambda x: len(x))
```

Here, min_val is being calculated using a lambda expression. Writing a lambda expression as a function duplicates the functionality of def, which violates the Python philosophy of doing things in one and only one way.

The PEP8 document says this regarding lambdas:

Always use a def statement instead of an assignment statement that binds a lambda expression directly to a name.

Yes:

*def f(x): return 2*x*

No:

*f = lambda x: 2*x*

The first form means that the name of the resulting function object is specifically 'f' instead of the generic '<lambda>'. This is more useful for tracebacks and string representations in general. The use of the assignment statement eliminates the sole benefit a lambda expression can offer over an explicit def statement (i.e. that it can be embedded inside a larger expression)

When to Use Generators vs. List Comprehension

The main difference between generators and list comprehension is that list comprehension keeps the data in memory while generators do not.

Use list comprehension in the following cases:

- When you need to iterate over the list multiple times.

- When you need to list methods to play with data that is not available in the generator

- When you don't have large data to iterate over and you think keeping data in memory won't be an issue

Let's say you want to get the line of a file from a text file, as shown in Listing 1-22.

Listing 1-22. Read File from a Document

```
def read_file(file_name):
"""Read the file line by line."""
    fread = open(file_name, "r")
    data = [line for line in fread if line.startswith(">>")]
    return data
```

31

Here, the file could be so big that having that many lines in a list could impact the memory and make your code slow. So, you might want to consider using an iterator over a list. See Listing 1-23 for an example.

Listing 1-23. Read a File from a Document Using Iterators

```
def read_file(file_name):
"""Read the file line by line."""
    with open(file_name) as fread:
        for line in fread:
            yield line

for line in read_file("logfile.txt"):
    print(line.startswith(">>"))
```

In Listing 1-23, instead of pushing data into memory using list comprehension, you are reading each line at a time and taking action. However, list comprehension can be passed around for further action to see whether it has found all the lines that start with >>>, while a generator needs to run each time to find the line that starts with >>>.

Both are great features of Python, and using them as described will make your code performant.

Why Not to Use else with Loops

Python loops have an else clause. Basically, you can have an else clause after Python for or while loops in your code. The else clause in the code runs only when control exits normally from the loop. If control exists in a loop with a break keyword, then control won't enter into the else section of code.

Having an else clause with loops is kind of confusing, which makes lots of developers avoid this feature. This is understandable considering the nature of the if/else condition in normal flow.

Let's look at the simple example in Listing 1-24; the code is trying to loop over a list and has an else clause outside and right after the loop.

Listing 1-24. else Clause with for Loop

```
for item in [1, 2, 3]:
    print("Then")
else:
    print("Else")
```

```
Result:
    >>> Then
    >>> Then
    >>> Then
    >>> Else
```

At first glance, you might think that it should print only three Then clauses and not Else as that would be skipped in a normal scenario of an if/else block. This is a natural way to look at the logic of the code. However, that assumption is not correct here. This gets more confusing if you use the while loop, as shown in Listing 1-25.

Listing 1-25. else Clause with the for Loop

```
x = [1, 2, 3]
while x:
    print("Then")
    x.pop()
else:
    print("Else")
```

The result is as follows:

```
>>> Then
>>> Then
>>> Then
>>> Else
```

Here the while loop runs until the list is not empty and then runs the else clause.

There is a reason to have this functionality in Python. One main use case could be to have an else clause right after the for and while loops to perform an additional action once the loop has ended.

Let's consider the example in Listing 1-26.

Listing 1-26. else Clause with break

```
for item in [1, 2, 3]:
    if item % 2 = 0:
        break
    print("Then")
else:
    print("Else")
```

The result is as follows:

```
>>> Then
```

However, there are better ways to write this code instead of using the else clause outside of the loop. You can use the else clause with the break in the loop or without the break condition. However, there are multiple ways to achieve the same result without using the else clause. You should use the condition instead of else in loops as there is a risk of misunderstanding the code by other developers, and it also a little harder to understand the code at a glance. See Listing 1-27.

Listing 1-27. else Clause with break

```
flag = True
for item in [1, 2, 3]:
    if item % 2 = 0:
        flag = False
        break
    print("Then")
if flag:
    print("Else")
```

Result is as follows:

```
>>> Then
```

This code makes it easier to read and understand, and there is no possibility of confusion while reading the code. The else clause is an interesting approach to writing code; however, it might impact the code's readability, so avoiding it might be a better way to solve the problem.

Why range Is Better in Python 3

If you have worked with Python 2, you might have used xrange. In Python 3, xrange has been renamed to range with some extra features. range is similar to xrange and generate an iterable.

```
>>> range(4)
range(0, 5)          # Iterable
>>> list(range(4))
[0, 1, 2, 3, 4]      # List
```

There are some new features in the range function of Python 3. The main advantage of having a range compared to a list is that it doesn't keep data in memory. Compared to lists, tuples, and other Python data structure, range represents an immutable iterable object that always takes the small and same amount of memory irrespective of the size of range because it only stores start, stop, and step values and calculates values as needed.

There are a couple of things you can do with range that are not possible in xrange.

- You can compare the range data.

```
>>> range(4) == range(4)
True
>>> range(4) == range(5)
False
```

- You can slice.

```
>>> range(10)[2:]
range(2, 10)
>>> range(10)[2:7, -1)
range(2, 7, -1)
```

range has lot of new features, which you can check out here for more detail: https://docs.python.org/3.0/library/functions.html#range.

Also, you can consider using range when you need to work on numbers instead of lists of numbers in your code because it will be much faster compared to lists.

It's also recommended that you use iterables in your loop as much as possible when you are dealing with numbers because Python gives you a method like range to do it easily.

Don't do this:

```
for item in [1, 2, 3, 4, 5, 6, 7, 8, 9, 10]:
    print(item)
```

Do this:

```
for item in range(10):
    print(item)
```

The first loop would be much costlier in term of performance, and if this list happens to be large enough, it would make your code much slower because of the memory situation and popping out the number from the list.

Raising Exceptions

Exceptions help you report errors in your code. In Python, exceptions are handled by a built-in module. It's important to have a good understanding of exceptions. Understanding when and where to use them will make your code less prone to errors.

Exceptions can expose errors in your code without much effort, so never forget to add exceptions in your code. Exceptions help consumers of your API or library understand the limitations of your code so they can put good error mechanisms to use while using your code. Raising an exception in the right place in your code immensely helps other developers to comprehend your code and makes third-party customers happy while using your API.

Frequently Raised Exceptions

You might wonder when and where to raise exceptions in your Python code.

I usually prefer to throw an exception whenever a fundamental assumption of the current code block is found to be false. Python prefers to have exceptions when you have a failure in your code. Even if you have a continuous failure, you want to raise an exception for it.

Let's consider that you need to divide two numbers in Listing 1-28.

Listing 1-28. Division of Numbers with Exceptions

```python
def division(dividend, divisor):
"""Perform arithmetic division."""
    try:
        return dividend/divisor
    except ZeroDivisionError as zero:
        raise ZeroDivisionError("Please provide greater than 0
        value")
```

As you can see in this code, you are raising an exception whenever you assume there might be a possibility of having errors in code. This helps the calling code to assure that the code will get an error whenever you have ZeroDivisionError in your code and handles it in different ways. See Listing 1-29.

Listing 1-29. Division Without Exceptions

```python
result = division(10, 2)
```

What happens if we return None here as:

```python
def division(dividend, divisor):
"""Perform arithmetic division."""
    try:
        return dividend/divisor
    except ZeroDivisionError as zero:
        return None
```

If the caller doesn't handle the case where calling on the division(dividend, divisor) method never fails even if you have ZeroDivisionError in your code, and if you are returning None from division(dividend, divisor) method in case of any exception, which could make difficult to diagnose in future when code size grows or the requirements changes. It's better to avoid returning None by division(divident, divisor) function in case of any failure or exception to make it easier for caller to understand what failed during the function execution. When we raise exception, we let caller know upfront that input values are not correct and need to provide the correct ones and we avoid any hidden bugs.

From a caller perspective, it's simply more convenient to get an exception rather than a return value, which is the Python style to indicate that there is a failure.

Python's credo is "It's easier to ask forgiveness than permission." This means that you don't check beforehand to make sure you won't get an exception; instead, if you get exception, you handle it.

Basically, you want to make sure that you raise an exception whenever you think there is a possibility of failure in your code so the calling class can handle them gracefully and not be taken by surprise.

In other words, if you think your code can't be run reasonably and hasn't figured out the answer yet, consider throwing an exception.

Leverage finally to Handle Exceptions

The code in finally always runs in Python. The finally keyword is useful while handling exceptions, especially when you are dealing with resources. You can use finally to make sure files or resources are closed or released, regardless of whether an exception has been raised. This is true even if you don't catch the exception or don't have specific exception to catch. See Listing 1-30.

Listing 1-30. finally Keyword Use

```
def send_email(host, port, user, password, email, message):
"""send email to specific email address."""
try:
```

```
        server = smtlib.SMTP(host=host, port=port)
        server.ehlo()
        server.login(user, password)
        server.send_email(message)
finally:
    server.quite()
```

Here you are handling the exception using `finally`, which helps to clean up the resources in a server connection, in case you have some kind of exception during login or in `send_email`.

You can use the `finally` keyword to write the block where you close the file, as shown in Listing 1-31.

Listing 1-31. finally Keyword Use to close the file

```
def write_file(file_name):
"""Read given file line by line"""
    myfile = open(file_name, "w")
    try:
        myfile.write("Python is awesome")        # Raise
                                                  TypeError
    finally:
        myfile.close()              # Executed before TypeError
                                    propagated
```

Here you are handling closing the file inside the `finally` block. Whether or not you have an exception, the code in `finally` will always run and close the file.

So, when you want to execute a certain code block irrespective of an exception being present, you should prefer to use `finally` to do that. Using `finally` will make sure you are handling your resources wisely and in addition will make your code cleaner.

Create Your Own Exception Class

When you are creating an API or library or are working on a project where you want to define your own exception to be consistent with the project or API, it's advisable to create your own exception class. This will help you immensely while you are diagnosing or debugging your code. It also helps to make your code cleaner because the caller will know why the error has been thrown.

Let's assume you have to raise exception when you can't find a user in a database. You want to make sure that the exception class name reflects the intention of the error. Having the name UserNotFoundError itself explains why you have an exception and the intention.

You can define your own exception class in Python 3+ as shown in Listing 1-32.

Listing 1-32. Creating a Specific Exception Class

```python
class UserNotFoundError(Exception):
"""Raise the exception when user not found."""
    def __init__(self, message=None, errors=None):
        # Calling the base class constructor with the parameter
        it needs
        super().__init__(message)
        # New for your custom code
        self.errors = errors

def get_user_info(user_obj):
"""Get user information from DB."""
    user = get_user_from_db(user_obj)
    if not user:
        raise UserNotFoundException(f"No user found of this id:
        {user_obj.id}")

get_user_info(user_obj)
>>> UserNotFoundException: No user found of this id: 897867
```

41

You also want to make sure that when you create your own exception class, those exception are descriptive and have well-defined boundaries. You'll want to use UserNotFoundException only in places where the code can't find a user, and you'll want to inform the calling code that the user information has not been found in the database. Having a specific set of boundaries for custom-defined exceptions makes it easier to diagnose the code. When you are looking at your code, you know exactly why the code has thrown that specific exception.

You can also define a broader scope for an exception class with naming, but the name should signify that it handles specific kinds of cases, as shown in Listing 1-33. The listing shows ValidationError, which you can use for multiple validation cases, but its scope is defined by all exceptions that are validation-related.

Listing 1-33. Creating a Custom Exception Class with a Broader Scope

```
class ValidationError(Exception):
"""Raise the exception whenever validation failed.."""
    def __init__(self, message=None, errors=None):
        # Calling the base class constructor with the parameter
        it needs
        super().__init__(message)
        # New for your custom code
        self.errors = errors
```

This exception has a much broader scope compared to UserNotFoundException. ValidationError can be raised whenever you think that validation has been failed or specific input does not have a valid input; however, the boundary is still defined by the validation context. So, make sure that you know the scope of your exception and raise an exception when an error is found in the scope of that exception class.

Handle Only Specific Exceptions

While catching the exception, it's recommended that you catch only specific exceptions instead of using the except: clause.

except: or except Exception will handle each and every exception, which can cause your code to hide critical bugs or exceptions which you don't intend to.

Let's take a look at the following code snippet, which uses the except clause in the try/catch block to call the function get_even_list.

Don't do this:

```
def get_even_list(num_list):
"""Get list of odd numbers from given list."""
    # This can raise NoneType or TypeError exceptions
    return [item for item in num_list if item%2==0]

numbers = None
try:
    get_even_list(numbers)
except:
    print("Something is wrong")

>>> Something is wrong
```

This kind of code hides an exception like NoneType or TypeError, which is obviously a bug in your code, and the client application or service will have a hard time figuring it out why they are getting message like "Something is wrong." Instead, if you raise a specific kind of exception with a proper message, the API client would be thankful to you for your diligence.

When you use except in your code, Python internally considers it as except BaseException. Having a specific exception helps immensely, especially in a larger code base.

Do this:

```
def get_even_list(num_list):
"""Get list of odd numbers from given list."""
    # This can raise NoneType or TypeError exceptions
    return [item for item in num_list if item%2==0]

numbers = None
try:
    get_even_list(numbers)
except NoneType:
    print("None Value has been provided.")
except TypeError:
    print("Type error has been raised due to non sequential
    data type.")
```

Handling a specific exception helps while debugging or diagnosing your issue. The caller will immediately know why the code has failed and will force you to add code to handle specific exceptions. This also makes your code less error prone for calling and caller code.

As per the PEP8 documentation, while handling exceptions, you should use the except keyword in these cases:

- When the exception handler will be printing out or logging the traceback. At least the user will be aware that an error has occurred in that case.

- When the code needs to do some cleanup work but then lets the exception propagate upward with raise. try...finally can be a better way to handle this case.

Note   Handling a specific exception is one of the best practices while writing code, especially in Python because it will help you save a lot of time while debugging the code. Also, it will make sure that your code fails fast instead hiding bugs in code.

Watch Out for Third-Party Exceptions

While calling a third-party API, it's really important that you are aware of all the kind of exceptions thrown by a third-party library. Getting to know all types of exceptions can help you to debug the issue later.

If you think that an exception don't quite suit your use case, consider creating your own exception class. While working with a third-party library, you can create your own exception class if you want to rename the exception name according to your application errors or want to add a new message in a third-party exception.

Let's take a look at the botocore client library in Listing 1-34.

Listing 1-34. Creating a Custom Exception Class with a Broader Scope

```
from botocore.exceptions import ClientError

ec2 = session.get_client('ec2', 'us-east-2')
try:
    parsed = ec2.describe_instances(InstanceIds=['i-badid'])
except ClientError as e:
    logger.error("Received error: %s", e, exc_info=True)
    # Only worry about a specific service error code
    if e.response['Error']['Code'] == 'InvalidInstanceID.NotFound':
        raise WrongInstanceIDError(message=exc_info, errors=e)

class WrongInstanceIDError(Exception):
```

```
"""Raise the exception whenever Invalid instance found."""
    def __init__(self, message=None, errors=None):
        # Calling the base class constructor with the parameter
        it needs
        super().__init__(message)
        # New for your custom code
        self.errors = errors
```

Consider two things here.

- Adding logs whenever you find a specific error in a third-party library will make it easier to debug issues in a third-party library.

- Here you defined a new error class to define your own exception. You might not want to do it for every exception; however, if you think that creating a new exception class will make your code cleaner and more readable, then consider creating a new class.

Sometimes it's hard to find the correct way to handle an exception thrown by a third-party library/API. Getting to know at least some of the common exceptions that are thrown by a third-party library will make it easier for you when battling production bugs.

Prefer to Have Minimum Code Under try

Whenever you handle an exception in your code, try to keep the code in a try block at a minimum. This makes it clear to other developers which part of the code is supposed to have a risk of throwing an error. Having a minimum of code or the code that has the potential to throw an exception in a try block also helps you to debug the issue more easily. Not having a try/catch block for exception handling might be slightly faster; however, if the exception is not handled, it might cause the application to fail. So, having good exception handling makes your code error free and can save you millions in production.

Let's look at an example.

Don't do this:

```
def write_to_file(file_name, message):
"""Write to file this specific message."""
    try:
        write_file = open(file_name, "w")
        write_file.write(message)
        write.close()
    except FileNotFoundError as exc:
        FileNotFoundException("Please provide correct file")
```

If you look closely at the previous code, you will see that there are opportunities to have different kinds of exceptions. One is `FileNotFound` or `IOError`.

You can use a different exception on one line or write a different exception in a different `try` block.

Do this:

```
def write_to_file(file_name, message):
"""Write to given file this specific message."""
    try:
        write_file = open(file_name, "w")
        write_file.write(message)
        write.close()
    except (FileNotFoundError, IOError) as exc:
        FileNotFoundException(f"Having issue while writing into
        file {exc}")
```

Even if there is no risk of having exceptions on other lines, it's preferable to write the minimum code in a `try` block as follows.

Don't do this:

```
try:
    data = get_data_from_db(obj)
    return data
except DBConnectionError:
    raise
```

Do this:

```
try:
    data = get_data_from_db(obj)
except DBConnectionError:
    raise
return data
```

This makes cleaner code and makes it clear that you are expecting an exception only while accessing the get_data_from_db method.

Summary

In this chapter, you learned some common practices that can help you to make your Python code more readable and simpler.

Additionally, exception handling is one of the most important parts of writing code in Python. Having a good understanding of exceptions helps you to maintain your application. This is especially true in big projects where you have more chances of having various kinds of production issues because of the different moving parts of an application being worked on by different developers. Having exceptions in the right places in your code can save you a lot of time and money, especially when you are debugging issues in production. Logging and exceptions are two of the most important parts of any mature software application, so planning ahead for them and considering them as a core part of software application development will help you write more maintainable and readable code.

CHAPTER 2

Data Structures

Data structures are the basic building blocks of any programming language. Having a good grasp of data structures saves you a lot of time, and using them can make your code maintainable. Python has a number of ways to store data using data structures, and having a good understanding of when to use which data structure makes a lot of difference in terms of memory, ease of use, and the performance of the code.

In this chapter, I will first go through some common data structures and explain when to use them in your code. I will also cover the advantages of using those data structures in specific situations. Then, you will consider in detail the importance of the dictionary as a data structure in Python.

Common Data Structures

Python has a number of primary data structures. In this section, you will look at the most common data structures. Having a good understanding of data structure concepts is important for you to write efficient code. Using them intelligently makes your code more performant and less buggy.

© Sunil Kapil 2019

S. Kapil, *Clean Python*, https://doi.org/10.1007/978-1-4842-4878-2_2

Use Sets for Speed

Sets are fundamental data structures in Python. They're also one of the most neglected ones. The main benefit of using sets is speed. So, let's look at some of the other characteristics of sets:

- They don't allow duplicates.

- You can't access set elements using an index.

- Sets can access elements in O(1) time since they use hashtables.

- Sets don't allow some common operations that lists do like slicing and lookups.

- Sets can sort the elements at insertion time.

Considering these constraints, whenever you don't need these common functionalities in your data structure, prefer to use a set, which will make your code a lot faster while accessing the data. Listing 2-1 shows an example of using a set.

Listing 2-1. Set Usage for Accessing Data

```
data = {"first", "second", "third", "fourth", "fifth"}
if "fourth" in data:
    print("Found the Data")
```

Sets are implemented using hashtables, so whenever a new item is added to a set, the positioning of the item in memory is determined by the hash of the object. That's the reason hashes are pretty performant while accessing the data. If you have thousands of items and you need to frequently access items from those elements, it's way faster to use sets to access items instead of using lists.

Let's look at another example (Listing 2-2) where sets are useful and can help make sure your data is not being duplicated.

Listing 2-2. Set Usage for Removing Duplicates

```
data = ["first", "second", "third", "fourth", "fourth",
"fifth"]
no_duplicate_data = set(data)
>>> {"first", "second", "third", "fourth", "fifth"}
```

Sets are also used as keys for dictionaries, and you can use sets as keys for other data structures such as lists.

Let's consider the example in Listing 2-3 where you have a dictionary from a database with an ID value as the key and the first and last names of users in values.

Listing 2-3. Sets as First and Last Names

```
users = {'1267':{'first': 'Larry', 'last':'Page'},
         '2343': {'first': 'John', 'last': 'Freedom'}}

ids = set(users.keys())
full_names = []
for user in users.values():
    full_names.append(user["first"] + "" + user["last"])
```

This gives your set of IDs and a list of full names. As you can see, sets can be derived from lists.

Note   Sets are useful data structures. Consider using them when you need to frequently access items from a list of numbers and set the access to the items in O(1) time. I recommend thinking about sets before considering using lists or tuples the next time you need a data structure.

Use namedtuple for Returning and Accessing Data

namedtuple is basically a tuple with the name of the data. namedtuple can do the same thing a tuple can but also has some extra features that a tuple doesn't have. With a namedtuple, it is easy to create a lightweight object type.

namedtuple makes your code more Pythonic.

Access the Data

Accessing the data using namedtuple makes it much more readable. Say you want to create a class whose values won't be changed after initializing. You might create a class like the one shown in Listing 2-4.

Listing 2-4. Immutable Class

```
class Point:
    def __init__(self, x, y, z):
        self.x = x
        self.y = y
        self.z = z

point = Point(3, 4, 5)
point.x
point.y
point.z
```

If you are not going to change the values of class Point and prefer to write them using namedtuple, it will make your code much more readable, as shown in Listing 2-5.

Listing 2-5. namedtuple Implementation

```
Point = namedtuple("Point", ["x", "y", "z"])
point = Point(x=3, y=4, z=5)
point.x
point.y
point.z
```

As you can see here, this code is much more readable and has fewer lines than using a normal class. Because a namedtuple uses the same memory as a tuple, they are as performant as tuples.

You might be wondering why you don't use a dict instead of namedtuple because they are easy enough to write.

Tuples are immutable, whether named or not. namedtuple makes the access more convenient by using names instead of indices. namedtuple has a stringent restriction in that field names have to be strings. Also, namedtuple doesn't perform any hashing because it generates a type instead.

Return the Data

Usually you would return data in a tuple. However, you should consider using namedtuple for returning data because it makes code more readable without much context. I would even suggest that whenever you are passing data from one function to another function, you should see whether you can use namedtuple because it makes your code much more Pythonic and readable. Let's consider the example in Listing 2-6.

Listing 2-6. Return a Value from a Function as a Tuple

```
def get_user_info(user_obj):
    user = get_data_from_db(user_obj)
    first_name = user["first_name"]
    last_name = user["last_name"]
```

```
    age = user["age"]
    return (first_name, last_name, age)

def get_full_name(first_name, last_name):
    return first_name + last_name

first_name, last_name, age = get_user_info(user_obj)
full_name = get_full_name(first_name, last_name)
```

So, what's the problem with this function? The issue is with returning the values. As you can notice, you are returning the values of first_name, last_name, and age of the user after fetching them from the database. Now, consider that you need to pass these values to some other function as get_full_name. You are passing these values around, and it's making visual noise for the reader to read your code. If you have more values to pass around like this, imagine how difficult it would be for a user to follow your code. It might have been nicer if you could bind these values to a data structure so that it provides the context without writing extra code.

Let's rewrite this code using namedtuple, which will make much more sense, as shown in Listing 2-7.

Listing 2-7. Return a Value from a Function as a Tuple

```
def get_user_info(user_obj):
    user = get_data_from_db(user_obj)
    UserInfo = namedtuple("UserInfo", ["first_name", "last_
    name", "age"])

    user_info = UserInfo(first_name=user["first_name"],
                         last_name=user["last_name"],
                         age=user["age"])

    return user_info

def get_full_name(user_info):
    return user_info.first_name + user_info.last_name
```

```
user_info = get_user_info(user_obj)
full_name = get_full_name(user_info)
```

Writing the code using namedtuple gives it context without you providing extra information with the code. Here user_info as namedtuple gives you that extra context without being explicitly set when returning from a function called get_user_info. Therefore, using namedtuple makes your code much more readable and maintainable in the long run.

If you have ten values to return, you might usually consider using tuple or dict while moving data around. Both of these data structures aren't very readable when data is being moved around. A tuple doesn't give any context or names to the data that is in tuple, and dict doesn't have unmutability, which constrains you when you don't want data to change after the first assignment. namedtuple fills both those gaps here.

Finally, if you want to convert namedtuple to a dict or convert a list to namedtuple, namedtuple gives you methods to do it easily. So, they are flexible as well. The next time you are creating a class with immutable data or returning multiple values, consider using namedtuple for the sake of readability and maintainability.

Note   You should use namedtuple instead of a tuple wherever you think object notation will make your code more Pythonic and readable. I usually consider them when I have multiple values to pass around with some kind of context; in these cases, namedtuple can fit the bill because it makes code much more readable.

Understanding str, Unicode, and byte

Understanding some of the fundamental concepts in the Python language will help you as a developer and make you a better programmer while handling data. Specifically, in Python, having a basic understanding of str,

Unicode, and byte helps you when you are working with data. Python is really easy to code for data processing or anything related to data because of its built-in library and its simplicity.

As you might already know, str is a representation type of a string in Python. See Listing 2-8.

Listing 2-8. Type str for Different Values

```
p = "Hello"
type(p)
>>> str

t = "6"
type(t)
>>> str
```

Unicode gives a unique identification to each character in almost all languages, such as the following:

```
0x59 : Y
0xE1 : á
0x7E : ~
```

The numbers assigned to characters by Unicode are called *code points*. So, what's the purpose of having Unicode?

The purpose of Unicode is to give a unique ID to each character for almost all languages. You can use the Unicode code point for any character, irrespective of the language. Unicode is usually formatted with a leading U+ and a then hexadecimal numeric value padded to at least four digits.

So, the thing you need to remember is that all Unicode does is to assign a numerical ID called a *code point* to each character so you have an unambiguous reference.

When you map any character to a bit pattern, it is called *encoding*. These bit patterns are used by the computer memory or on disk. There are multiple ways you can encode the characters; the most common are ASCII, ISO-8859-1, and UTF-8.

Python interpreters use UTF-8 for encoding.

So, let's briefly talk about UTF-8. UTF-8 maps all Unicode characters to bit patterns of length 8, 16, 24, or 32, which is 1, 2, 3, or 4 correspondingly.

As an example, a will be converted by the Python interpreter to 01100001, and å will be converted to 11000011 01011111 (0xC3 0xA1). So, it's easy to understand why Unicode is useful.

Note   In Python 3, all strings are a sequence of Unicode characters. So, you should not be thinking about encoding strings to UTF-8 or decoding from UTF-8 to strings. You can still convert a string to bytes and bytes back to a string using string-encoding methods.

Use Lists Carefully and Prefer Generators

Iterators are really useful, especially when you are handling a large amount of data. I have seen code where people use a list to store sequence data but then there is risk of memory leak affecting the performance of your system.

Let's consider the example in Listing 2-9.

Listing 2-9. Using a List of Return Prime Numbers

```
def get_prime_numbers(lower, higher):
    primes = [ ]
    for num in range(lower, higher + 1):
        for prime in range(2, num + 1):
            is_prime = True
            for item in range(2, int(num ** 0.5) + 1):
```

```
            if num % item == 0:
                is_prime = False
                break

    if is_prime:
        primes.append(num)
print(get_prime_numbers(30, 30000))
```

What's the problem with code like this? First, it's hard to read, and second, it could be dangerous in terms of memory leak because you are storing large numbers in memory. How can you make this code better in terms of readability and performance?

This is where you can consider using generators, which use yield keys to generate numbers, and you can use them as an iterator to pop out the values. Let's rewrite this example using iterators, as shown in Listing 2-10.

Listing 2-10. Using Generators for Prime Numbers

```
def is_prime(num):
    for item in range(2, int(math.sqrt(num)) + 1):
        if num % item == 0:
            prime = False
    return prime

def get_prime_numbers(lower, higher):
    for possible_prime in range(lower, higher):
        if is_prime(possible_prime):
            yield possible_prime
        yield False

for prime in get_prime_numbers(lower, higher):
    if prime:
        print(prime)
```

This code is much more readable and performant. Also, a generator unintentionally forces you to think about refactoring your code. Here returning values in a list makes the code much more bloated, which the generator solves easily.

One of the common cases that I have observed is that iterators can be really useful when you are getting data from a database and you don't know how many rows you will be fetching. This could be memory-intensive work as you might try to save those values in memory. Instead, try using an iterator, which would return a value right away and go to the next row to give the next value.

Let's say you have to access a database to get a user's age and name by ID. You know the IDs that are indexes in the database, and you know the total number of users in the database, which is 1,000,000,000. Mostly I have seen code where a developer tries to get data in a chunk using a list, which is an OK approach to solve memory issues. Listing 2-11 shows an example of this.

Listing 2-11. Access a Database and Store the Result in a List as a Chunk

```python
def get_all_users_age(total_users=1000):
    age = []
    for id in total_users:
        user_obj = access_db_to_get_users_by_id(id)
        age.append([user.name, user.age])
    return age

total_users = 1000000000
for user_info in range(total_users):
    info = get_all_users_age()
    for user in info:
        print(user)
```

Here you are trying to get the user's age and name by accessing the database. However, this approach might not be good when you don't have much memory in the system because you are randomly picking a number that you consider memory-safe to store user information, but you can't guarantee that. Python provides a generator as a solution to avoid these issues and tackle these situations in your code. You can consider rewriting it as shown in Listing 2-12.

Listing 2-12. Using an Iterator Approach

```
def get_all_users_age():
    all_users = 1000000000
    for id in all_users:
        user_obj = access_db_to_get_users_by_id(id)
        yield user.name, user.age

for user_name, user_age in get_all_users_age():
    print(user_name, user_age)
```

Note   Generators are a useful feature of Python because they make your code performant for data-intensive work. A generator also forces you to think about making the code readable.

Use zip to Process a List

When you have two lists and you want to process them in parallel, consider using zip. This is a built-in function of Python and very efficient.

Let's assume you have a user's name and salary in a user table in the database, and you would like to combine them into another list and return that as a list for all users. You have the functions get_users_name_from_db and get_users_salary_from_db, which give you a list of users and the corresponding salary of users. How can you combine them? One of the ways to do this is shown in Listing 2-13.

Listing 2-13. Combine a List

```python
def get_user_salary_info():
    users = get_users_name_from_db()
    # ["Abe", "Larry", "Adams", "John", "Sumit", "Adward"]

    users_salary = get_users_salary_from_db()
    #  ["2M", "1M", "60K", "30K", "80K", "100K"]

    users_salary = []
    for index in len(users):
        users_salary.append([users[index], users_salary[index]])

    return users_salary
```

Is there a better way to solve this problem? Of course. Python has a built-in function called zip that handles this part easily for you, as shown in Listing 2-14.

Listing 2-14. Using zip

```python
def get_user_salary_info():
    users = get_users_name_from_db()
    # ["Abe", "Larry", "Adams", "John", "Sumit", "Adward"]

    users_salary = get_users_salary_from_db()
    #  ["2M", "1M", "60K", "30K", "80K", "100K"]

    users_salary = []
    for usr, slr in zip(users, users_salary):
        users_salary.append(usr, slr)

    return users_salary
```

If you have a lot of data, consider using an iterator here instead of storing into a list. `zip` makes it easier to combine two lists and process them in parallel, so using `zip` will allow you to do these jobs efficiently.

Take Advantage of Python's Built-in Functions

Python has lots of built-in libraries that are pretty awesome. I can't go into each library in this chapter as there are lots of them. I will cover some basic data structure libraries that can make a big impact on your code and improve your code quality.

collections

This is one of the most widely used libraries and has useful data structures, specifically `namedtuple`, `defaultdict`, and `orderddict`.

csv

Use `csv` for reading and writing CSV files. It will save you lot of time instead of writing your own methods while reading files.

datetime and time

These are without a doubt two of the most used libraries. In fact, you have probably already encountered them. If not, getting familiar with the different methods available in these libraries is beneficial in different scenarios, especially when you are working with timing issues.

math

The `math` lib has lots of useful methods to perform basic to advanced math computations. Before looking for a third-party library to solve math problems, try to see whether this library already has them.

re

There is no substitute for this library that can solve problems using regular expressions. In fact, re is one of the best libraries in the Python language. If you know regular expressions well, you can create magic using the re library. It gives you the power to perform some of the more difficult operations easily using regular expressions.

tempfile

Consider this a one-off library to create temporary files. It's a good built-in library.

itertools

Some of the most useful tools in this library are permutations and combinations. However, if you explore it more, you will find that you can solve a lot of computation problems using itertools. It has some of the useful functions such as dropwhile, product, chain, and islice.

functools

If you are developer who loves functional programming, this library is for you. It has lots of functions that will help you to think of your code in a more functional way. One of the most used partials is in this library.

sys and os

Use these libraries when you want to perform any specific system- or OS-level operations. sys and os give you the power to do a lot of amazing things with your system.

subprocess

This library helps you to create multiple processes on your system without much effort. The library is easy to use, and it creates multiple processes and handles them using multiple methods.

logging

No big project could be successful without a good logging feature. The logging library from Python helps you to easily add logging in your system. It has different ways to spit out logs such as the console, files, and the network.

json

JSON is the de facto standard for passing information over a network and for APIs. The json library from Python does a great job of handling different scenarios. The json library interface is easy to use, and the documentation is pretty good.

pickle

You might not use it in daily coding, but whenever you need to serialize and deserialize a Python object, there is no better library than pickle.

__future__

This is a pseudomodule that enables new language features that are not compatible with the current interpreter. So, you might want to consider using them in your code where you want to use a future version. See Listing 2-15.

Listing 2-15. Using __future__

```
import __future__ import division
```

Note   Python has rich libraries that solve a lot of problems for you. Getting to know them is the first step to figuring out what they can do for you. Familiarizing yourself with the built-in Python libraries will help you in the long run.

Now that you've explored some of the most common data structures in Python, let's dig more into one of the most commonly used data structures in Python: the dictionary. If you are writing professional Python code, you will definitely use a dictionary, so let's learn more about them!

Take Advantage of Dictionary

A dictionary is one of the most used data structures in Python. Dictionaries are a faster way to access the data. Python has elegant built-in libraries for dictionaries, which also makes them easy to use. In this section, you will look closely at some of the most useful features of dictionaries.

When to Use a Dictionary vs. Other Data Structures

When you are considering something that can map the data, it might be time to consider a dictionary as the data structure in your code.

If you are storing data that needs some kind of mapping and you need to access it fast, then using a dictionary would be wise; however, you don't want to consider using a dictionary for each data store.

So, as an example, consider the case when you need an extra mechanism of a class or need an object, or consider using a tuple or namedtuple when you need immutability in your data structure. Think about which specific data structure you will need while you build your code.

collections

collections is one of the useful modules in Python. It's a high-performance data type. collections has a number of interfaces that are really useful for performing different tasks with dictionary. So, let's look at some of the main tools in collections.

Counter

Counter gives you a convenient way to tally up similar data. As an example, see Listing 2-16.

Listing 2-16. Counter

```
from collections import Counter

contries  = ["Belarus", "Albania", "Malta", "Ukrain",
"Belarus", "Malta", "Kosove", "Belarus"]
Counter(contries)
>>> Counter({'Belarus': 2, 'Albania': 1, 'Malta': 2, 'Ukrain':
1, 'Kosove': 1})
```

Counter is a dict subclass. It's an order collection where elements are stored as dictionary keys and their tallies are stored as values. This is one of the most efficient ways to count the numbers of values. Counter has multiple useful methods. most_common(), as the name suggests, returns the most common element and its count. See Listing 2-17 for an example.

Listing 2-17. most_count() Method in Counter

```
from collections import Counter

contries  = ["Belarus", "Albania", "Malta", "Ukrain",
"Belarus", "Malta", "Kosove", "Belarus"]
contries_count = Counter(contries)
```

```
>>> Counter({'Belarus': 2, 'Albania': 1, 'Malta': 2, 'Ukrain':
1, 'Kosove': 1})
contries_count.most_common(1)
>>> [('Belarus', 3)]
```

Other methods such as elements() return an iterator with the element repeating as many times as the count.

deque

If you want to create a queue and stack, then consider using deque. It allows you to append values from left to right. deque also supports thread-safe, memory-efficient appends and pops from either side with the same O(1) performance.

deque has methods such as append(x) to append to the right side, appendleft(x) to append to the left side, clear() to remove all elements, pop() to remove elements from the right side, popleft() to remove from the left side, and reverse() to reverse the element. Let's look at some of the cases. See Listing 2-18.

Listing 2-18. deque

```
from collections import deque

# Make a deque
deq = deque("abcdefg")

# Iterate over the deque's element
[item.upper() for item in deq]
>>> deque(["A", "B", "C", "D", "E", "F", "G"])

# Add a new entry to right side
deq.append("h")
>>> deque(["A", "B", "C", "D", "E", "F", "G", "h"])
```

```
# Add an new entry to the left side
deq.appendleft("I")
>>> deque(["I", "A", "B", "C", "D", "E", "F", "G", "h"])

# Remove right most element
deq.pop()
>>> "h"

# Remove leftmost element
deq.popleft()
>>> "I"

# empty deque
deq.clear()
```

defaultdict

A defaultdict works like dict because it's a subclass of dict. A defaultdict is initialized with function("default factory"), which takes no argument and provides the default value for a nonexistent key. defaultdict doesn't raise a KeyError like dict. Any key that doesn't exist gets the value returned by the default factory.

Let's take a look at the simple example in Listing 2-19.

Listing 2-19. defaultdict

```
from collections import defaultdict

# Make a defaultdict
colors = defaultdict(int)

# Try printing value of non-existing key would give us default
values
colors["orange"]
>>> 0
```

```
print(colors)
>>> defaultdict(int, {"orange": 0})
```

namedtuple

One of the most popular tools is namedtuple in a collection module. It's a subclass of tuple with a named field and fixed length. namedtuple can be used wherever you used a tuple in your code. namedtuple is an immutable list and makes it easier to read the code and access the data.

I've already discussed namedtuple, so refer to that discussion to learn more about it.

ordereddict

ordereddict can be used when you want to get the keys in a specific order. dict doesn't give you the order as the insertion order, which is ordereddict's main feature. In Python 3.6+, dict also has this feature where dict is by default ordered by the insertion order.

So, as an example, see Listing 2-20.

Listing 2-20. OrderedDict

```
from collections import ordereddict

# Make a OrderedDict
colors = OrderedDict()

# Assing values
colors["orange"] = "ORANGE"
colors["blue"] = "BLUE"
colors["green"] = "GREEN"

# Get values
[k for k, v in colors.items()]
>>> ["orange", "blue", "green"]
```

Ordered Dictionary vs. Default Dictionary vs. Normal Dictionary

I touched on some of these topics in earlier sections. Now let's look closely some different types of dictionaries.

The OrderedDict and DefaultDict dictionary types are subclasses of the dict class (a normal dictionary) with some added features to make them distinguishable from dict. However, they possess all the same features as a normal dictionary. There is a reason for these dictionary types in Python, and I will talk about where these different dictionaries can be used to make best use of these libraries.

As of Python 3.6, dicts are now ordered by insertion order, which actually reduces the usefulness of ordereddict.

Let's now talk about OrderedDict for pre-3.6 Python versions. OrderedDict gives you orderly values as you insert them into the dictionary. Sometimes in your code you might want to access data in an orderly fashion; this is where you can use OrderedDict. OrderedDict doesn't have any extra cost compared to a dictionary, so performance-wise both are the same.

Say you want store when a programming language was first introduced. You could use OrderedDict to fetch the information of the language as you insert that language information by their founding year, as shown in Listing 2-21.

Listing 2-21. OrderedDict

```
from collections import OrderedDict

# Make a OrderedDict
language_found = OrderedDict()

# Insert values
language_found ["Python"] = 1990
```

```
language_found ["Java"] = 1995
language_found ["Ruby"] = 1995

# Get values
[k for k, v in langauge_found.items()]
>>> ["Python", "Java", "Ruby"]
```

Sometimes you want to have default values assigned to keys when you access or insert keys in a dictionary. In a normal dictionary, you would get KeyError if the key doesn't exist. However, defaultdict will create the key for you. See Listing 2-22.

Listing 2-22. defaultdict

```
from collections import defaultdict

# Make a defaultdict
language_found = defaultdict(int)

# Try printing value of non-existing key
language_found["golang"]
>>> 0
```

Here when you call DefaultDict and try to access the golang key, which doesn't exist, internally defaultdict will call the function object (which is int in the language_found case), which you have passed in the constructor. It's a callable object, which includes function and type objects. So, int and list that you passed are functions into defaultdict. When you try to access the key, which doesn't exist, it calls the function that has been passed and assigns its return value as the value of the new key.

As you already know, a dictionary is a key-value collection in Python. Lots of advanced library like defaultdict and OrderedDict are being built on top of the dictionary to add some new features that don't have extra cost in terms of performance. dict for sure will be slightly faster; however, most of the cases will have a negligence difference. So, consider using them when writing your own solution for these problems.

switch Statement Using Dictionary

Python doesn't have a switch keyword. However, Python has lots of features that can make this functionality possible in a cleaner way. You can leverage dictionary to make a switch statement, and also you should consider writing the code this way whenever you have multiple options to choose from based on specific criteria.

Consider a system that calculates the taxes of each county by that particular country's tax rules. There are multiple ways to do this; however, the most difficult part of having multiple options is not adding multiple if else conditions in your code. Let's see how can you solve this problem using dictionary in a more elegant way. See Listing 2-23.

Listing 2-23. switch Statement Using a Dictionary

```python
def tanzania(amount):
    calculate_tax = <Tax Code>
    return calculate_tax

def zambia(amount):
    calculate_tax = <Tax Code>
    return calculate_tax

def eritrea(amount):
    calculate_tax = <Tax Code>
    return calculate_tax

contry_tax_calculate = {
        "tanzania": tanzania,
            "zambia": zambia,
        "eritrea": eritrea,
}
```

```python
def calculate_tax(country_name, amount):
    country_tax_calculate["contry_name"](amount)
```

```python
calculate_tax("zambia", 8000000)
```

Here you simply use a dictionary to calculate the tax, which makes your code more elegant and much more readable compared to using a typical `switch` statement.

Ways to Merge Two Dictionaries

Say you have two dictionaries that you want to merge. Doing this is much simpler in Python 3.5+ compared to previous versions. Merging any two data structures is tricky because you need to be careful about memory use and loss of data while merging data structures. If you use extra memory to save the merged data structure, you should be aware of the memory limitations of your system considering the data size in your dictionary.

Losing data is also one concern. You might find that some of the data has been lost because of a restriction on a specific data structure; for example, in a dictionary, you can't have duplicate keys. So, keep these things in mind whenever you perform merge operations between dictionaries.

In Python 3.5+, you can do this as shown in Listing 2-24.

Listing 2-24. Merge Dictionaries in Python 3.5+

```python
salary_first = {"Lisa": 238900, "Ganesh": 8765000, "John":
3450000}
salary_second = {"Albert": 3456000, "Arya": 987600}
{**salary_first, **salary_second}
>>> {"Lisa": 238900, "Ganesh": 8765000, "John": 345000,
"Albert": 3456000, "Ary": 987600}
```

However, in pre-3.5 Python, you can do this with a little bit of extra work. See Listing 2-25.

Listing 2-25. Merge Dictionaries in Pre-3.5 Python

```
salary_first = {"Lisa": 238900, "Ganesh": 8765000, "John":
3450000}
salary_second = {"Albert": 3456000, "Arya": 987600}
salary = salary_first.copy()
salary.update(salary_second)
>>> {"Lisa": 238900, "Ganesh": 8765000, "John": 345000,
"Albert": 3456000, "Ary": 987600}
```

Python 3.5+ has PEP 448, which has proposed extended uses of the * iterable unpacking operator and the ** dictionary unpacking operators.

This definitely makes the code more readable. This not only applies to dictionaries but also to lists since Python 3.5.

Pretty Printing a Dictionary

Python has a module called pprint so you can print nicely. You need to import pprint to perform the operation.

pprint gives you the option to provide indentation while you print any data structure. Indentation will be applied to your data structure. See Listing 2-26.

Listing 2-26. pprint for a Dictionary

```
import pprint

pp = pprint.PrettyPrinter(indent=4)
pp.pprint(colors)
```

This might not work as expected for complicated dictionaries that are more nested and have a lot of data. You can consider using JSON for this, as shown in Listing 2-27.

Listing 2-27. Using json to Print Dictionaries

```
import json

data = {'a':12, 'b':{'x':87, 'y':{'t1': 21, 't2':34}}
json.dumps(data, sort_keys=True, indent=4)
```

Summary

Data structures are the core of every programming language. As you learned while reading this chapter, Python offers a number of data structures to store and manipulate the data. Python gives you all kinds of tools in the form of data structures to perform all kinds of operations on different kinds of objects or data sets. As a Python developer, it's important to be aware of different kinds of data structures so you can make the right decision while writing your application, especially in an application that is resource-intensive.

I hope this chapter has helped make you aware of some of the most useful data structures in Python. Getting familiar with different kinds of data structures with their different behavior makes you a better developer because you can have different kinds of tools in your toolkit.

CHAPTER 3

Writing Better Functions and Classes

Functions and classes are core parts of the Python language. All the code you write in the professional world consists of functions and classes. In this chapter, you will learn about best practices that will help to make your code more readable and cleaner.

While writing functions and classes, it's important you think about the boundaries and structures of your functions/classes. Having a clear understanding of the use cases that your function or class is trying to solve will help you to write better classes and functions. Always keep in mind the philosophy of the single responsibility principle.

Functions

As you know, everything in Python is an object, and functions are no exception. Functions in Python are very flexible, so it is important to make sure you write them carefully. I will discuss some best practices while writing functions in Python.

© Sunil Kapil 2019
S. Kapil, *Clean Python*, https://doi.org/10.1007/978-1-4842-4878-2_3

In Python, typically when you write blocks of code in the def clause, you will define them as functions or methods. I'm not talking about lambda functions here as I already covered them in earlier chapters.

Create Small Functions

Always prefer to write a function that does one and only one task. How do you make sure that your function is doing only one operation, and how do you measure the size of your function? Do you consider lines or characters a measure of function size?

Well, it's more about tasks. You want to make sure your function is doing only one task, but that task could be built on top of multiple subtasks. As a developer, you must decide when you want to break down a subtask into separate functions. Nobody can answer those questions for you. You must critically analyze your function and decide when to break them down to multiple functions. This is a skill you have to acquire by continuously analyzing your code and looking for places in your code that "smell," or in other words are hard to read and comprehend.

Consider the real-world example in Listing 3-1.

Listing 3-1. Unique E-mail Example

```python
def get_unique_emails(file_name):
    """
    Read the file data and get all unique emails.
    """
    emails = set()
    with open(file_name) as fread:
            for line in fread:
                match = re.findall(r'[\w\.-]+@[\w\.-]+', line)
                for email in match:
                    emails.add(email)
    return emails
```

In Listing 3-1, get_unique_emails is performing two different tasks, first looping over a given file to read each line and second performing a regex to match e-mails on each line. You might have observed two things here: first is of course the number of tasks that are performed by the function and second that you can you break this down further and make a general function that reads file or reads lines. You can break this function into two distinct functions, where one can read a file and the second can read lines. So, as a developer, it's up to you to decide whether this function needs to be broken down to write cleaner code. See Listing 3-2.

Listing 3-2. Breaking Functions into Different Functions

```python
def get_unique_emails(file_name):
    """
    Get all unique emails.
    """

    emails = set()
    for line in read_file(file_name):
        match = re.findall(r'[\w\.-]+@[\w\.-]+', line)
        for email in match:
            emails.add(email)
    return emails

def read_file(file_name):
    """
    Read file and yield each line.
    """

    with open(file_name) as fread:
        for line in fread:
            yield line
```

In Listing 3-2, function `read_file` is now a generic function that can accept any file name and `yield` each line, and `get_unique_emails` performs the action on each line to find unique e-mails.

Here, I have created `read_file` as a generator function. However, if you want it to return a list, you can consider doing that. The main idea is that you should break down a function after considering readability and the single responsibility principle.

Note   I recommend that you first write the code that implements the functionality, and once you have implemented the feature and it works, you can start thinking about breaking the function into multiple functions for clearer code. Also, remember to follow good naming conventions.

Return Generators

As you might have noticed in the code example of Listing 3-2, I used `yield` instead of using any specific data structure like `list` or `tuple`. The main reason to not use any other data structure here is that you are not sure how big the file could be and there is a possibility of running out of memory when processing big files.

Generators are functions that use the `yield` keyword (as shown in Listing 1-22 of Chapter 1), and `read_file` is a generator function. Generators are useful for two main reasons.

- When generators call functions, they immediately return the iterator instead of running the whole function, on which you can perform different actions like looping or converting to a list (in Chapter 1's Listing 1-22, you loop over iterator). Once you are done, it automatically calls the built-in function `next()` and goes back to the calling function read_file on the next line after the yield keyword. It also makes your code easier to read and understand.

- In a list or another data structure, Python needs to save the data in memory before returning, which can cause a memory crash if the data turns out to be large. A generator does not have this issue. So, when you have a large amount of data to process or you are not sure about the data size beforehand, it is recommended to use a generator instead of another data structure.

Now you can consider making some changes in Listing 3-2's get_unique_emails function code and use yield instead of a list, as shown in Listing 3-3.

Listing 3-3. Breaking a Function into Different Functions

```python
def get_unique_emails(file_name):
    """

    Get all unique emails.
    """

    for line in read_file(file_name):
        match = re.findall(r'[\w\.-]+@[\w\.-]+', line)
        for email in match:
            yield email

def read_file(file_name):
    """

    Read file and yield each line.
    """

    with open(file_name) as fread:
        for line in fread:
            yield line
```

```python
def print_email_list():
    """

    Print list of emails
    """

    for email in get_unique_emails('duplicate_emails'):
        print(email)
```

Here you omit the risk of sending all the e-mails in the list from the get_unique_emails function.

I am not implying here that you should use generators in every return function. If you know beforehand that you need to return only a specific data size, it might be easier to use a list/tuple/set/dict instead. As an example, in Chapter 1's Listing 1-22, if you are returning 100 e-mails, it is better to use a list or some other data structure instead of using a generator. However, in cases where you are unsure about the data size, consider using generators, which will save you lot of production memory issues.

Note   Familiarize yourself with Python generators. I haven't see a lot of developers using generators in professional code, but you should consider their advantages. It makes your code cleaner and saves you from memory issues.

Raise Exceptions Instead of Returning None

I talked about exceptions at length in Chapter 1, so I will not be talking about all the exception cases here. This section deals only with raising exceptions when you have errors instead of returning None from functions.

Exceptions are a core feature of Python. There are a couple of things that need to be considered while using exceptions.

First, I have noticed that a lot of programmers either return None or log something when anything unexpected happens in the code. Sometimes this strategy can be dangerous because it can hide bugs.

Also, I have seen code where a function returns None or some random values instead of raising an exception, which makes your code confusing for the caller function as well as error prone. See Listing 3-4.

Listing 3-4. Return None

```python
def read_lines_for_python(file_name, file_type):
    if not file_name or file_type not in ("txt", "html"):
        return None

    lines = []
    with open(file_name, "r") as fileread:
        for line in fileread:
            if "python" in line:
                return "Found` Python"

If not read_lines_for_python("file_without_python_name",
"pdf"):
    print("Not correct file format or file name doesn't exist")
```

In Listing 3-4, you cannot be sure if read_lines_for_python returns None because the file does not have any Python word or file issue. This kind of code can lead to unexpected bugs in your code, and it could be headache to find bugs in a big codebase.

So, whenever you are writing code and have a situation where you are returning None or some other values because something unexpected happens, consider raising an exception. It will save you time chasing down bugs as your code gets bigger.

Consider writing this code as shown in Listing 3-5.

Listing 3-5. Raising an Exception Instead of None

```python
def read_lines_for_python(file_name, file_type):
    if file_type not in ("txt", "html"):
        raise ValueError("Not correct file format")
    if not file_name:
        raise IOError("File Not Found")

    with open(file_name, "r") as fileread:
    for line in fileread:
            if "python" in line:
                return "Found Python"

If not read_lines_for_python("file_without_python_name",
"pdf"):
    print("Python keyword doesn't exists in file")

Result:  >> ValueError("Not correct file format")
```

Whenever your code fails, you know by looking at the exception why it's failing. Raising an exception helps you to catch bugs early instead of guessing.

Note   Python is a dynamic language, so you need to be careful while writing the code, especially when you find an unexpected value in your code. None is the default value returned from a function, but don't overuse it for every unexpected situation. Think about whether you can raise an exception to make your code cleaner before using None.

Add Behavior Using the default and keyword Arguments

Keyword arguments are useful for making your Python code more readable and cleaner. Keyword arguments are used to supply a default value to a function or can be used as a keyword. See Listing 3-6.

Listing 3-6. Default Arguments

```python
def calculate_sum(first_number=5, second_number=10):
    return first_number + second_number

calculate_sum()
calculate_sum(50)
calculate_sum(90, 10)
```

Here you have used a keyword argument to define default values, but while calling a function, you can choose if you need default or user-defined values.

The usefulness of a keyword argument is significant in a large codebase or a function with multiple arguments. Keyword arguments help to make the code easier to understand.

So, let's look at an example where you need to find spam e-mails by using a keyword in the e-mail content, as shown in Listing 3-7.

Listing 3-7. Without Keyword Arguments

```python
def spam_emails(from, to, subject, size, sender_name, receiver_
name):
    <rest of the code>
```

If you are calling spam_emails without any keyword arguments, it looks like Listing 3-8.

Listing 3-8. Without Keyword Arguments

```
spam_emails("ab_from@gmail.com",
            "nb_to@yahoo.com",
            "Is email spam",
            10000,"ab", "nb")
```

If you only investigate the line in Listing 3-8, it's hard to guess what all these parameters mean to a function. If you see that many parameters are used to call a function, for readability it's better to use keyword arguments to call a function, as shown in Listing 3-9.

Listing 3-9. With Keyword Arguments

```
spam_emails(from="ab_from@gmail.com",
            to="nb_to@yahoo.com",
            subject="Is email spam",
            size=10000,
            sender_name="ab",
            receiver_name="nb")
```

This is not an absolute rule, but consider using keyword arguments for more than two function parameters. Using keyword arguments for a calling function makes your code more understandable for new developers.

In Python 3+, you can force a keyword argument into a caller function by defining a function as follows:

```
def spam_email(from, *, to, subject, size, sender_name,
receiver_name)
```

Do Not Return None Explicitly

Python functions by default return None when you don't return explicitly. See Listing 3-10.

Listing 3-10. Default None Return

```
def sum(first_number, second_number):
    sum = first_number + second_number

sum(80, 90)
```

Here function sum returns None by default. However, many times people write code that explicitly returns None in the function, as shown in Listing 3-11.

Listing 3-11. Return None Explicitly

```
def sum(first_number, second_number):
    if isinstance(first_number, int) and isinstance(second_
    number, int):
        return first_number + second_number
    else:
        return None

result = sum(10, "str")            # Return None
result = sum(10, 5)                # Return 15
```

Here you expect the result to be a value in the sum function, which is misleading because it could return None or a sum of two numbers. So, you always need to check the result for None, which is too much noise in the code and makes the code more complex over time.

You might want to raise an exception in these cases. See Listing 3-12.

Listing 3-12. Raise an Exception Instead of Returning None

```
def sum(first_number, second_number):
    if isinstance(first_number, int) and isinstance(second_
    number, int):
        return first_number + second_number
    else:
        raise ValueError("Provide only int values")
```

87

Let's look at a second example, shown in Listing 3-13, where you are returning None explicitly if a given input is not a list.

Listing 3-13. Return None Explicitly

```
def find_odd_number(numbers):
    odd_numbers = []
    if isinstance(numbers, list):
        return None
    for item in numbers:
        if item % 2 != 0:
            odd_numbers.append(item)
    return odd_numbers

num = find_odd_numbers([2, 4, 6, 7, 8, 10])        # return 7
num = find_odd_numbers((2, 4, 6, 7, 8, 10))        # return None
num = find_odd_number([2, 4, 6, 8, 10])            # return []
```

This function by default returns None if it does not find an odd number. The function also returns None if the type of numbers is not a list.

You can consider rewriting this code, as shown in Listing 3-14.

Listing 3-14. Not Returning None Explicitly

```
def find_first_odd_number(numbers):
    odd_numbers = []
    if isinstance(numbers, list):
        raise ValueError("Only accept list, wrong data type")
    for item in numbers:
        if item % 2 != 0:
            odd_numbers.append(item)
    return odd_numbers
```

```
num = find_odd_numbers([2, 4, 6, 7, 8, 10])      # return 7
num = find_odd_numbers((2, 4, 6, 7, 8, 10))      # Raise ValueError
                                                 exception
num = find_odd_number([2, 4, 6, 8, 10])          # return []
```

Now when you check the num value, you know the exact reason of having [ ] in your function call. Explicitly adding this makes sure that the reader knows what to expect when no odd number is found.

Be Defensive While Writing a Function

We programmers are fallible, so there is no guarantee that you will not make a mistake when you write code. Considering this fact, you can take creative measures while writing a function that can prevent or expose bugs in your code before going to production or help you find them even in production.

There are two things that you as a programmer can do before shipping code off to production to make sure that you are shipping quality code.

- Logging

- Unit test

Logging

Let's talk about logging first. Logging can help immensely when you try to debug the code, especially in production when you do not know beforehand where things might have gone wrong. In any mature project, especially medium to large ones, it would be difficult to keep the project maintainable for a long time without logging. Having logging in your code makes code much easier to debug and diagnose when a production issue arises.

Let's look how logging code typically looks, as shown in Listing 3-15. This is one of the many ways to write logging in Python.

Listing 3-15. Logging in Python

```python
# Import logging module
Import logging

logger = logging.getLogger(__name__)          # Create a custom
                                               logger
handler = logging.StreamHandler                # Using stream
                                               handler

# Set logging levels
handler.setLevel(logging.WARNING)
handler.setLevel(logging.ERROR)

format_c = logging.Formatter("%(name) - %(levelname) -
%(message)")
handler.setFromatter(format_c)                 # Add formater to
                                               handler

logger.addHandler(handler)

def division(divident, divisor):
    try:
        return divident/divisor
    catch ZeroDivisionError:
        logger.error("Zero Division Error")

num = divison(4, 0)
```

Python has a `logging` module that is comprehensive and customizable. You can define a different level of logging in your code. If your project has a different type of error, you can log that error as per the severity of the situation. For example, the severity of an exception during user account creation would be higher than a failure when sending a marketing e-mail.

The Python `logging` module is a mature library that gives you plenty of features to configure logging per your needs.

Unit Test

Unit tests are one of the most important parts of your code. Professionally, making unit tests mandatory in your code can prevent you from introducing bugs and can give you a sense of confidence over your code before you push to production. There are lots of great libraries in Python that make it easier to write unit tests. Some of the popular ones are the py. test and unittest libraries. We talked about them in detail in Chapter 8. This is how it looks when writing unit tests in Python:

unittest

```
import unittest

def sum_numbers(x, y):
    return x + y

class SimpleTest(unittest.TestCase):
    def test(self):
        self.assertEqual(sum_numbers(3, 4), 7)
```

py.test

```
def sum_numbers(x, y):
    return x + y

def test_sum_numbers():
    assert func(3, 4) == 7
```

A unit test can play some key roles when you write it properly.

- You can use a unit test as documentation for the code, which can be immensely helpful when you revisit your code or new developers join the project.

- It can give you a sense of confidence in your code that it does the expected behavior. When you have tests for your functions, you can make sure that any changes in the code do not break the function.

- It can prevent old bugs from creeping into your code since you are running your unit test before pushing to production.

Some developers go beyond unit test by writing the code in test-driven development (TDD), but this does not mean only TDD should have a unit test. Every project that needs to be used by users should have unit tests.

Note   In any mature project, logging and unit testing are must-haves. They can help you immensely to prevent bugs in your code. Python gives you a library called `logging`, which is pretty mature. For unit testing, Python has plenty of options to choose from. `pytest` and `unittest` are popular options.

Use a Lambda as a Single Expression

Lambdas are interesting features in Python, but I advise you to avoid them. I have seen plenty of code where lambdas are overused or misused.

PEP8 suggests *not* to write the code shown in Listing 3-16.

Listing 3-16. Lambda

```
sorted_numbers = sorted(numbers, key=lambda num: abs(num))
```

Instead, write the code as shown in Listing 3-17.

Listing 3-17. Using a Normal Function

```
def sorted_numbers(numbers):
    return sorted(numbers, reverse=True)
```

There are couple of reason to avoid lambdas.

- They make the code harder to read, which is more important than having a one-line expression. For example, the following code makes lots of developers uneasy about lambdas:

  ```
  sorted(numbers, key=lambda num: abs(num))
  ```

- Lambda expressions are easily misused. Often developers try to make code clever by writing a one-line expression, which makes it difficult to follow for other developers. And in the real world, it can cause more bugs in your code. See Listing 3-18.

Listing 3-18. Misuse of Lambda Functions

```
import re
data = [abc0, abc9, abc5, cba 2]
convert = lambda text: float(text) if text.isdigit() else text
alphanum = lambda key: [convert(c) for c in re.spl
it('([-+]?[0-9]*\.?[0-9]*)', key) ]
data.sort( key=alphanum )
```

In Listing 3-18, the code is misusing lambda functions, and it is harder to understand then if a function were used.

I suggest using a lambda in the following cases:

- When everyone on your team understands the lambda expression

- When it makes your code more understandable than using functions

- When the operations you are doing are trivial and the function does not need a name

Classes

Next, I will discuss classes.

Right Size of Class?

If you are doing object-oriented programming in any language, you might wonder what the right size of a class is.

While writing a class, always remember the single responsibility principle (SRP). If you are writing a class that has a clearly defined responsibility with clearly defined boundaries, you should not worry about a line of class code. Some people believe one class with one file is a good measure of a class; however, I have seen code where the file itself is noticeably big, and it could be confusing and misleading to see one class per file. If you see that a class is doing more than one thing, that means it's the right time to create a new class. Sometimes it's a fine line in terms of responsibility; however, you have to be careful when you are adding a new code in a class. You don't want to cross the boundaries of responsibilities.

Looking at each method and line of code carefully and thinking about whether that method or part of code fits into the class's overall responsibility is a good way to investigate the class structure.

Let's say you have a class called UserInformation. You don't want to add the payment information and order information of each user to this class. Even if the information related to the user is not necessary user information, payment information and order information are more of activities of users with payments. You want to make sure these responsibilities are defined before writing a class. You can define that the UserInformation class is responsible for keeping the state of the user information, not user activities.

Duplicate code is another hint that a class might be doing more than it is supposed to do. As an example, if you have a class called Payment and you are writing ten lines of code to access a database that includes creating a connection with a database, getting user information, and getting user credit card information, you might want to consider creating another class just to access a database. Then any other class can use this class to access a database without duplicating the same code or method everywhere.

I suggest having a clear definition of class scope before writing code and sticking with a class scope definition will solve most class size problems.

Class Structure

I prefer a class structure in this order:

1. Class variables

2. __init__

3. Built-in Python special methods (__call__, __repr__, etc.)

4. Class methods

5. Static methods

6. Properties

7.   Instance methods

8.   Private methods

As example, you might want to have code that looks like Listing 3-19.

Listing 3-19. Class Structure

```
class Employee(Person):
    POSITIONS = ("Superwiser", "Manager", "CEO", "Founder")

    def __init__(self, name, id, department):
        self.name = name
        self.id = id
        self.department = department
        self.age = None
        self._age_last_calculated = None
        self._recalculated_age()

    def __str__(self):
        return ("Name: " + self.name + "\nDepartment: "
                + self.department)

    @classmethod
    def no_position_allowed(cls, position):
        return [t for t in cls.POSITIONS if t != position]

    @staticmethod
    def c_positions(position):
        return [t for t in cls.TITLES if t in position]

    @property
    def id_with_name(self):
        return self.id, self.name
```

```
def age(self):
    if (datetime.date.today() > self._age_last_recalculated):
        self.__recalculated_age()
    return self.age

def _recalculated_age(self):
    today = datetime.date.today()
    age = today.year - self.birthday.year
    if today < datetime.date(
        today.year, self.birthday.month,
        self.birthday.year):
        age -= 1
    self.age = age
    self._age_last_recalculated = today
```

Class Variables

Usually you want to see a class variable at the top because these variables either are constants or are default instance variables. This shows a developer that these constant variables are ready to use, so this is valuable information to keep at the top of the class before any other instance method or constructor.

__init__

This is a class constructor, and the calling method/class needs to know how to access the class. __init__ represents a door for any class that tells how to call the class and which states are in the class. __init__ also gives you information about the class's main input to supply before starting to use the class.

Special Python Methods

Special methods change the default behavior of a class or give extra functionality to class, so having them at the top of a class makes the reader of the class aware of some customized features of the class. Also, these metaclasses that are being overridden give you an idea that a class is trying to do something different by changing the usual behavior of the Python class. Having them at the top allows the user to keep the modified behavior of the class in mind before reading the rest of the class code.

Class Methods

A class method works as another constructor, so keeping it near __init__ makes sense. It tells the developer other ways the class can be used without creating a constructor using __init__.

Static Methods

A static method is bound to the class and not the object of the class like class methods. They can't modify the class state, so it makes sense to add them at the top to make the reader aware of the methods that are used for specific purposes.

Instance Methods

Instance methods add behavior in a class, so it's expected by a developer that if a class has a certain behavior, then the instance method would be part of the class. Therefore, keeping them after special methods makes it easier for a reader to understand the code.

Private Methods

As Python doesn't have any private keyword concept, using _<name> in the method name tells the reader that this is a private method so don't use it. You can keep it at the bottom with the instance methods.

I suggest keeping private methods around instance methods to make it easier for the reader to understand the code. You can have private methods before the instance method and vice versa; it's all about calling the method nearest to the called method.

Note   Python is an object-oriented language, and it should be treated as such when you are writing classes in Python. Following all the rules of OOP will not harm you. While writing classes, make sure that it is easy for the reader to understand the class. Instance methods should be next to each other if one of the methods is using another method. The same goes for private methods.

Right Ways to Use @property

The @property decorator (discussed in Chapter 5) is one of the useful features of Python for getting and setting values. There are two places you can consider using @property in a class: in complex code hidden behind an attribute and in the validation of the set attribute. See Listing 3-20.

Listing 3-20. Class Property Decorator

```python
class Temperature:
    def __init__(self, temperature=0):
        self.temperature = temperature

    @property
    def fahrenheit(self):
        self.temperature = (self.temperature * 1.8) + 32
```

```
temp = Temperature(10)
temp.fahrenheit
print(temp.temperature)
```

What's the problem with this code? You are using a property decorator in the method fahrenheit, but the method updates the self.temperature variable value instead of returning any value. When you use a property decorator, make sure you return the value; this will make it easier for the calling class/method to expect something returned from method when you use a property decorator. So, make sure you return the value and use a property decorator method as a getter in your code, as shown in Listing 3-21.

Listing 3-21. Class Property Decorator

```
class Temperature:
    def __init__(self, temperature=0):
        self.temperature = temperature

    @property
    def fahrenheit(self):
        return (self.temperature * 1.8) + 32
```

A property decorator is also used for validating/filtering the values. It's the same as a setter in other programming languages like Java. In Python, you can validate/filter specific pieces of information using a property decorator. I have seen a lot of places where developers usually don't realize the power of the setter property decorator in Python. Using it in a proper way makes your code readable and will save you from those corner bugs that you sometimes forget.

In Listing 3-22 is an example of implementing validation using a property decorator in Python. It makes the code readable for a developer and easy to understand by showing what to validate when you set a specific value.

In this example, you have a class called Temperature that sets the temperature in Fahrenheit. Using a property decorator to get and set the value of the temperature makes it easier for the Temperature class to validate the caller input.

Listing 3-22. Class Property Decorator

```
class Temperature:
    def __init__(self, temperature=0):
        self.temperature = temperature

    @property
    def fahrenheit(self):
        return self._temperature

    @fahrenheit.setter
    def fahrenheit(self, temp):
        if not isinstance(temp, int):
            raise("Wrong input type")

        self._temperature = (self.temp * 1.8) + 32
```

Here, the fahrenheit setter method does the validation part before calculating the temperature in Fahrenheit, which makes the calling class expect that an exception could be raised in the case of wrong input. The calling class now gets the value of Fahrenheit by just calling the fahrenheit method without any input.

Always make sure that you use property keywords in the right context and consider them as the getter and setter of writing code in a Pythonic way.

When to Use Static Methods?

By definition, static methods are related to classes but don't need to access any class-specific data. You don't use self or cls in a static method. These methods can work on their own without having any dependency on the class state. This is one of the main reasons for getting confused when using static methods instead of stand-alone functions.

When you write a class in Python, you want to group similar kinds of methods but also keep a specific state by using methods that use different variables. Also, you want to perform different actions using objects of the class; however, when you make a method static, this method doesn't have access to any of the class states and doesn't need object or class variables to access them. So, when should you use static methods?

When you are writing a class, there might a method that can live alone as a function and doesn't need class state to perform a specific action. Sometimes it makes sense to make that as a static method as part of a class. You can use this static method as a utility method for a class to use. But why don't you just make that a stand-alone function outside of the class? You can obviously do that, but keeping it inside the class makes it easier for the reader to relate that function with a class. Let's understand this using a simple example, as shown in Listing 3-23.

Listing 3-23. Without a Static Method

```
def price_to_book_ratio(market_price_per_share, book_value_per_
share):
    return market_price_per_share/book_value_per_share

class BookPriceCalculator:
    PER_PAGE_PRICE = 8

    def __init__(self, pages, author):
        self.pages = pages
        self.author = author
```

```
@property
def standard_price(self):
    return self.pages * PER_PAGE_PRICE
```

Here the method price_to_book_ratio can work without using any state of BookPriceCalculator, but it might make sense to keep it inside class BookPriceCalculator as it's related to the BookPricing class. So, you can write this code as shown in Listing 3-24.

Listing 3-24. With a Static Method

```
class BookPriceCalculator:
    PER_PAGE_PRICE = 8

    def __init__(self, pages, author):
        self.pages = pages
        self.author = author

    @property
    def standard_price(self):
        return self.pages * PER_PAGE_PRICE

    @staticmethod
    def price_to_book_ratio(market_price_per_share, book_value_
    per_share):
        return market_price_per_share/book_value_per_share
```

Here you make made it as a static method, and you do not need to use any of the class methods or variables, but it's related to the BookPriceCalculator class, so make it a static method.

Use Abstract Class Inheritance the Pythonic Way

Abstraction is one of the cool features of Python. It helps to make sure that an inherited class is implemented in an expected way. So, what is the main purpose of having an abstract class in your interface?

- You can make an interface class using abstraction.

- It can make it impossible to use an interface without implementing abstract methods.

- It gives early errors if you do not adhere to abstract class rules.

These benefits might violate the OOPS abstraction rules if you implement abstraction in python wrong way. Listing 3-25 shows the code that makes an abstract class without fully using the Python abstraction feature.

Listing 3-25. Abstract Class the Wrong Way

```python
class Fruit:
    def taste(self):
        raise NotImplementedError()

    def originated(self):
        raise NotImplementedError()

class Apple:
    def originated(self):
        return "Central Asia"

fruit = Fruit("apple")
fruit.originated                        #Central Asia
fruit.taste
NotImplementedError
```

So, the issues are as follows:

- You can initialize the class Apple or Fruit without getting any error; it should have thrown an exception as soon as you created an object of the class.

- The code might have gone into production without you even realizing that it's an incomplete class, until you use the taste method.

So, what is a better way to define an abstract class in Python so it fulfills the requirement of an ideal abstract class? Python solves this problem by giving you a module called abc, which does what you expect from an abstract class. Let's re-implement the abstract class using the abc module, as shown in Listing 3-26.

Listing 3-26. Abstract Class the Right Way

```
from abc import ABCMeta, abstractmethod

class Fruit(metaclass=ABCMeta):

    @abstractmethod
    def taste(self):
        pass

    @abstractmethod
    def originated(self):
        pass

class Apple:
    def originated(self):
        return "Central Asia"
```

```
fruite = Fruite("apple")
TypeError:
"Can't instantiate abstract class concrete with abstract method
taste"
```

Using the abc module makes sure that you implement all the expected methods, gives you maintainable code, and makes sure there is no half-baked code in production.

Use @classmethod to Access Class State

A class method gives you the flexibility to create alternative constructors besides using the __init__ method.

So, where you could utilize a class method in your code? As mentioned, an obvious place would be to create multiple constructors by passing a class object, so it's one of the easiest ways to create a factory pattern in Python.

Let's consider a scenario where you expect multiple-format input from calling methods and you need to return a standardize value. A serialization class is a good example here. Consider you have a class where you need to serialize a User object and return the user's first and last names. The challenge, however, is to make sure that the interface for the client is easier to use and the interface could get one of the four different formats: string, JSON, object, or file. Using the factory pattern might be effective way to solve this problem, and this is where the class method could be useful. Listing 3-27 shows an example.

Listing 3-27. Serialization Class

```
class User:

    def __init__(self, first_name, last_name):
        self.first_name = first_name
        self.last_name = last_name
```

```python
    @classmethod
    def using_string(cls, names_str):
        first, second = map(str, names_str.split(""))
        student = cls(first, second)
        return Student

    @classmethod
    def using_json(cls, obj_json):
        # parsing json object...
        return Student

    @classmethod
    def using_file_obj(cls, file_obj):
        # parsing file object...
        return Student

data = User.using_string("Larry Page")
data = User.using_json(json_obj)
data = User.using_file_obj(file_obj)
```

Here you create a User class and multiple class methods that behave like an interface for the client class to access a specific class state based on the client data.

A class method is a useful feature when you are building a big project with multiple classes, and having clean interfaces helps to keep code maintainable in the longer term.

Use the public Attribute Instead of private

As you know, Python doesn't have any private attribute concept for classes. However, you might have used or seen the code that uses the dunder _<var_name> variable name to mark a method as private. You can still access those variables, but doing that is considered prohibited, so it's been consensus among the Python community to consider the dunder _<var_name> variable or method as private.

Considering this fact, I still suggest refraining from using it everywhere you want to constrain your class variable as it could make your code cumbersome and brittle.

Let's says you have the class Person with _full_name as a private instance variable. To access the _full_name instance variable, you have created a method called get_name, which gives the caller class access to the variable without directly accessing the private method. See Listing 3-28.

Listing 3-28. Using _ in the Wrong Places

```python
class Person:

    def __init__(self, first_name, last_name):
        self._full_name = f"${first_name} ${last_name}"

    def get_name(self):
        return self._full_name

per = Person("Larry", "Page")
assert per.get_name() == "Larry Page"
```

However, this is still a wrong way to make a variable private.

As you can see, the Person class is trying to hide an attribute by naming it as _full_name; however, it makes the code much more cumbersome and hard to read, even if the intention of the code is to restrain user to accessing the _full_name variable only. This can make your code complex if you are considering doing this for every other private variable. Imagine what will happen if you have lots of private variables in your class and you have to define as many methods as private variables.

Make class variables or methods private, whenever you don't want to expose them to the caller class or method, as python doesn't enforce the private access to variable and methods, so by making class variable and methods private is a way to communicate caller class or method that these method or variables shouldn't be access or override.

I suggest using __<var_name> names in your code when you are trying to inherit some public class and you don't have control over that public class and its variable. When you want to avoid the conflict in the code, it's still a good idea to use __<var_name> to avoid name-mangling issues. Let's consider the simple example in Listing 3-29.

Listing 3-29. Using __ in Inheritance of a Public Class

```
class Person:

    def __init__(self, first_name, last_name):
        self.age = 50

    def get_name(self):
        return self.full_name

class Child(Person):

    def __init__(self):
        super().__init__()
        self.__age = 20

ch = Child()
print(ch.get())          # 50
print(ch.__age)          # 30
```

Summary

Python doesn't have any access control over the variables/methods or classes like some other programming languages such as Java. However, the Python community has come to a consensus for some of the rules including the private and public concept, even though Python considers everything public. You should also know when to use those features and when to avoid them so that your code is readable and looks eloquent to other developers.

CHAPTER 4

Working with Modules and Metaclasses

Modules and metaclasses are important features of Python. When working on large projects, having a good understanding of modules and metaprogramming will help you write cleaner code. Metaclasses in Python are a kind of hidden feature that you don't need to care about until you have a specific need to use them. Modules help you to organize your code/project and help you to structure your code.

Modules and metaclasses are big concepts, so explaining them here in detail would be difficult. In this chapter, you will explore some good practices regarding modules and metaprogramming.

Modules and Metaclasses

Before starting, I'll briefly explain the module and metaclass concepts in the Python world.

Modules are simply Python files with the `.py` extension. The name of the module will be the name of the file. A module could have a number of functions or classes. The idea of a module in Python is to logically separate the functionality of your project, as shown here:

```
users/
users/payment.py
users/info.py
```

© Sunil Kapil 2019
S. Kapil, *Clean Python*, https://doi.org/10.1007/978-1-4842-4878-2_4

payment.py and info.py are modules that logically separate the user's payment and information functionality. Modules help to make your code easier to structure.

Metaclasses are a big topic, but in short, they are a blueprint for the creation of a class. In other words, classes create an instance, and metaclasses help to change the class behavior automatically based on what's needed when it's created.

Let's assume that you need to create all the classes in your module starting with awesome. You can use __metaclass__ at the module level to do that. See Listing 4-1 for an example.

Listing 4-1. Metaclass Example

```
def awesome_attr(future_class_name, future_class_parents,
future_class_attr):
    """

    Return a class object, with the list of its attribute
    prefix with awesome keyword.
    """

    # pick any attribute that doesn't start with '__' and
    prefix with awesome
    awesome_prefix = {}
    for name, val in future_class_attr.items():
        if not name.startswith('__'):
            uppercase_attr["_".join("awesome", name)] = val
        else:
            uppercase_attr[name] = val

    # let `type` do the class creation
    return type(future_class_name, future_class_parents,
    uppercase_attr)

__metaclass__ = awesome_attr # this will affect all classes in
the module
```

```
class Example: # global __metaclass__ won't work with "object"
though
    # but we can define __metaclass__ here instead to affect
    only this class
    # and this will work with "object" children
    val = 'yes'
```

__metaclass__ is one of the features among a number of metaclass concepts. There are multiple metaclasses provided by Python that you can leverage per your needs. You can check them out at https://docs. python.org/3/reference/datamodel.html

Let's now look at some good practices to follow in Python while you are writing your code and considering using metaclasses or building modules.

How Modules Can Help to Organize Code

In this section, you will look at how modules can help you organize your code. Modules help separate code by holding related functions, variables, and classes. In other words, Python modules give you a tool to abstract different layers of your project by placing them into different modules.

Let's say you need to build an e-commerce web site where users can buy products. To build this kind of project, you might want to create different layers with specific purposes. At a high level, you might consider having layers for user actions, such as selecting a product, adding products to a cart, and making a payment. All these layers might have only one function or a couple of functions, which you can keep in one file or different files. When you want to use a lower level of a layer like a payment module in another module like adding products to the cart, you can do this by simply using the import statement as from ... import in the adding to the cart module.

Let's look at some of the rules that can help to create better modules.

- Keep your module name short. You can also consider not using an underscore or at least keep it minimal.

Don't do this:

```
import  user_card_payment
import add_product_cart
from user import cards_payment
```

Do this:

```
import payment
import cart
from user.cards import payment
```

- Avoid using names with a dot (.), uppercase, or some other special character. So, a file name like `credit. card.py` should be avoided. Having these kinds of special characters in the names creates confusion for other developers and can negatively affect the readability of the code. PEP8 also recommends not using these special characters for naming.

Don't do this:

```
import user.card.payment
import USERS
```

Do this:

```
import user_payment
import users
```

- When considering the readability of the code, it's important to import the modules in a certain way.

Don't do this:

```
[...]
from user import *
[...]
cart = add_to_cart(4)  # Is add_to_cart part of user? A
builtin? Defined above?
```

Do this:

```
from user import add_to_cart
[...]
x = add_to_cart(4)  # add_to_cart may be part of user,
if not redefined in between
```

Even better, do this:

```
import user
[...]
x = user.add_to_cart(4)  # add_to_cart is visibly
part of module's namespace
```

Being able to say where from a module comes from helps in readability, as shown in the previous example, where user.add_to_cart helps to identify where the add_to_cart function resides.

Making good use of modules can help your project achieve the following goals:

- **Scoping**: It helps you to avoid collisions between identifiers in different parts of the code.

- **Maintainability**: Modules help you to define logical boundaries in your code. If you have too many dependencies in your code, it would be hard for developers to work in a big project without modules. Modules help you to define those boundaries and minimize the dependency by segregating interdependent code in one module. This helps in large projects so many developers can contribute without stepping on each other's toes.

- **Simplicity**: Modules help you to break down big problems into smaller pieces, which makes it much easier to write code and makes it more readable for other developers. It also helps to debug the code and make it less error prone.

- **Reusability**: This is one of the main advantages of having modules. Modules can be easily used in different files such as libraries and APIs within the project.

At the end of the day, modules help to organize your code. Especially in big projects where multiple developers are working on different parts of the codebase, it is immensely important to have modules defined carefully and logically.

Take Advantage of the __init__ File

Since Python 3.3, __init__.py is not required to indicate that a directory is a Python package. Before Python 3.3, it was required to have an empty __init__.py file to make a directory a package. However, the __init__.py file can be useful in multiple scenarios to make your code easy to use and to package it in a certain way.

One of the main uses of __init__.py is to help split modules into multiple files. Let's consider the scenario where you have a module called purchase, which has two different classes named as Cart and Payment. Cart adds the product into the cart, and the Payment class performs the payment operation for the product. See Listing 4-2.

Listing 4-2. Module Example

```
# purchase module

class Cart:
    def add_to_cart(self, cart, product):
        self.execute_query_to_add(cart, product)

class Payment:
    def do_payment(self, user, amount):
        self.execute_payment_query(user, amount)
```

Suppose you want to split these two different functionalities (adding to the cart and the payment) into different modules to better structure the code. You can do that by moving the Cart and Payment classes into two different modules, as follows:

```
purchase/
    cart.py
    payment.py
```

You might consider coding the cart module as shown in Listing 4-3.

Listing 4-3. Cart Class Example

```
# cart module

class Cart:
    def add_to_cart(self, cart, product):
        self.execute_query_to_add(cart, product)
        print("Successfully added to cart")
```

Consider the payment module, as shown in Listing 4-4.

117

Listing 4-4. Payment Class Example

```
# payment module

class Payment:
    def do_payment(self, user, amount):
        self.execute_payment_query(user, amount)
        print(f"Payment of ${amount} successfully done!")
```

Now you can keep these modules in the __init__.py file to glue it together.

```
from .cart import Cart
from .payment import Payment
```

If you follow these steps, you have given a common interface to the client to use different functionality in your package as follows:

```
import purchase
>>> cart = purchase.Cart()
>>> cart.add_to_cart(cart_name, prodct_name)
Successfully added to cart
>>> payment = purchase.Payment()
>>> payment.do_payment(user_obj, 100)
Payment of $100 successfully done!
```

The primary reason to have modules is to create better-designed code for your client. Instead of the client dealing with multiple small modules and figuring out what feature belongs to which module, you can use a single module to deal with the different features of project. This is especially helpful in large code and third-party libraries.

Consider a client using your module as follows:

```
from  purchase.cart import Cart
from purchase.payment import Payment
```

This works, but it places more burden on the client to figure out what resides where in your project. Instead, unify things and allow single imports to make it easier for a client to use the module.

```
from purchase import Cart, Payment
```

In the latter case, it's most common to think of a large amount of source code as a single module. For example, in the previous line, purchase could be considered as a single piece of source code or a single module by the client, without worrying about where the Cart and Payment classes resides.

This also shows how to stitch together different submodules into a single module. As shown in the previous example, you can break large modules into different logical submodules, and the user can use only a single module name.

Import Functions and Classes from Modules in the Right Way

There are different ways to import classes and functions from the same or different modules in Python. You can import a package inside the same package, or you can import a package from outside of a package. Let's take a look at both scenarios to see which is the best way to import classes and functions from within a module.

- Inside packages, importing from the same package can be done using the fully specified path or relative path. Here's an example.

  Don't do this:

  ```
  from foo import bar            # Don't Do This
  ```

Do this:

```
from . import bar                    # Recommended way
```

The first import syntax is using the full path of the package such as TestPackage.Foo, and the name of the top-level package is hard-coded in the source code. The problem is if you want to change the name of the package or reorganize the directory structure of your project.

For example, if you ever want to change the name from TestPackage to MyPackage, you have to change the name in every place it appears. This can be brittle and hard to do if you have a lot of files in your project. It also makes it difficult for anyone to move the code. However, a relative import doesn't have this problem.

- Outside of a package, there are different ways to import a package from outside of a module.

```
from mypackage import *            # Bad
from mypackage.test import bar     # OK
import mypackage                   # Recommended way
```

The first option to import everything is obviously not the right way to import packages because you don't know what's being imported from the package. The second option is verbose and a good practice as it's explicit and much more readable compared to the first option.

The second option also helps the reader to understand what's being imported from which package. This helps to make the code more readable for other developers and helps them understand all the dependencies. However, an issue comes up when you have to import different packages from different places. This becomes a kind of noise in your code. Imagine if you have 10 to 15 lines of code for importing specific things from different packages. The second problem that I have noticed when you have the same name in different packages is that while writing code it creates a lot of confusion about which class/function belongs to which package. Here's an example:

```
from mypackage import foo
from youpackage import foo
foo.get_result()
```

The reason behind recommending a third option is that it's much more readable and gives you an idea while reading the code which classes and functions belong to which packages.

```
import mypackage
import yourpackage
mypackage.foo.get_result()
import yourpackage.foo.feed_data()
```

Use __all__ to Prevent Imports

There is one mechanism to prevent the user of your module from importing everything. Python has a special metaclass class called __all__, which allows you to control the behavior of an import. By using __all__, you can restrict consumer classes or methods to import only specific classes or methods instead of everything from the module.

As an example, consider that you have a module called user.py.
By defining __all__ here, you can restrict other modules to allow only
specific symbols.

Let's say you have a module called payment, where you keep all the
payment classes, and you want to prevent some of the class from importing
from this module by mistake. You can do that by using __all__, as shown
in the following example.

payment.py

```
class MonthlyPayment:

    ....

class CalculatePayment:

    ....

class CreditCardPayment:

    ....

__all__ = ["CalculatePayment", "CreditCardPayment"]
```

user.py

```
from payment import *

calculate_payment = CalculatePayment()        # This throw
                                               exception
monthly_payment = MonthlyPayment()             # This will work
```

As you might have noticed, using from payment import * doesn't
make all the classes of payment import automatically. However, you can
still import the CalculatePayment and CreditCardPayment classes by
specifically importing them as follows:

```
from payment import CalculatePayment
```

When to Use Metaclasses

As you know, metaclasses create classes. Just like you can create classes in order to create objects, in the same way Python metaclasses create these objects. In other words, metaclasses are classes' classes. As this section is not about how metaclasses work, I will focus on when you should consider using metaclasses.

Most of the time you won't need metaclasses in your code. The main use case of a metaclass is to create an API or library or add some complex feature. Whenever you want to hide a lot of detail and make it easier for the client to use your API/library, metaclasses can be really helpful to do that.

Take, for example, Django ORM, which heavily uses metaclasses to make its ORM API easy to use and understand. Django makes this possible by using metaclasses, and you write the Django ORM as shown in Listing 4-5.

Listing 4-5. __init__.py

```python
class User(models.Model):
    name = models.CharField(max_length=30)
    age = models.IntegerField()

user = User(name="Tracy", age=78)
print(user.age)
```

Here `user.age` won't return `IntegerField`; it will return an `int`, which it takes from a database.

Django ORM works because of the way the `Model` class leverages metaclasses. The `Model` class defines `__metaclass__`, and it uses some magic to turn the `User` class into a complex hook into the database field. Django makes something complex look simple by exposing a simple API and using metaclasses. Metaclasses make this possible behind the scenes.

There are different metaclasses like `__call__`, `__new__`, etc. All these metaclasses can help you to build beautiful APIs. If you look at the source

code of a good Python library such as flask, Django, requests, etc., you
will find that these libraries are using metaclasses to make their API look
easy to use and understand.

Consider using metaclasses whenever you find that using the normal
Python functionality won't make your API readable. Sometimes you have
to write boilerplate code using metaclasses to make your API easy to use.
I will discuss in a later section how metaclasses can be helpful in writing
cleaner API/libraries.

Use __new__ for Validating Subclasses

The magic method __new__ will be called when an instance is being
created. Using this method, you can easily customize the instance
creation. This method is called before calling __init__ while initializing
the instance of the class.

You can also create a new instance of a class by invoking the
superclass's __new__ method using super. Listing 4-6 shows an example.

Listing 4-6. __new__

```python
class User:
    def __new__(cls, *args, **kwargs):
        print("Creating instances")
        obj = super(User, cls).__new__(cls, *args, **kwargs)
        return obj

    def __init__(self, first_name, last_name):
        self.first_name = first_name
        self.last_name = last_name

    def full_name(self):
        return f"{self.first_name} {self.last_name}"
```

```
>> user = User("Larry", "Page")
Creating Instance
user.full_name()
Larry Page
```

Here, when you create an instance of the class, __new__ is called before calling the __init__ magic method.

Imagine a scenario where you have to create a superclass or abstract class. Whichever class inherits that superclass or abstract class should do the specific check or work, which is easy to forget or can be done incorrectly by the subclass. So, you might want to consider having that functionality in a superclass or abstract class, which also makes sure that every class has to adhere to those validation checks.

In Listing 4-7 you can use the __new__ metaclass to validate before any subclass inherits the abstract or superclass.

Listing 4-7. __new__ for Assigning a Value

```
from abc import abstractmethod, ABCMeta

class UserAbstract(metaclass=ABCMeta):
"""Abstract base class template, implementing factory pattern
using __new__() initializer."""

    def __new__(cls, *args, **kwargs):
    """Creates an object instance and sets a base property."""
        obj = object.__new__(cls)
        obj.base_property = "Adding Property for each subclass"
        return obj

class User(UserAbstract):
"""Implement UserAbstract class and add its own variable."""

    def __init__(self):
        self.name = "Larry"
```

125

```
>> user = User()
>> user.name
Larry
>> user.base_property
Adding Property for each subclass
```

Here, base_property automatically gets assigned the value "Adding Property for each subclass" whenever an instance is created for a subclass.

Now, let's modify this code to validate if provided value is string or not. See Listing 4-8.

Listing 4-8. __new__ for Validating the Provided Value

```
from abc import abstractmethod, ABCMeta

class UserAbstract(metaclass=ABCMeta):
"""Abstract base class template, implementing factory pattern
using __new__() initializer."""

    def __new__(cls, *args, **kwargs):
    """Creates an object instance and sets a base property."""
        obj = object.__new__(cls)
        given_data = args[0]
        # Validating the data here
        if not isinstance(given_data, str):
            raise ValueError(f"Please provide string: {given_
            data}")
        return obj

class User(UserAbstract):
"""Implement UserAbstract class and add its own variable."""

    def __init__(self, name):
        self.name = Name
```

126

```
>> user = User(10)
ValueError: Please provide string: 10
```

Here you validate that provided data is string whenever a value is being passed to create an instance for the User class. The real beauty of this is using the __new__ magic method without each subclass to do the duplicate work.

Why __slots__ Are Useful

__slots__ helps you save space in objects and get faster attribute access. Let's quickly test the performance of __slots__ with the simple example in Listing 4-9.

Listing 4-9. __slots__ Faster Attribute Access

```python
class WithSlots:
"""Using __slots__ magic here."""
    __slots__ = "foo"

class WithoutSlots:
"""Not using __slots__ here."""
    pass

with_slots = WithSlots()
without_slots = WithoutSlots()

with_slots.foo = "Foo"
without_slots.foo = "Foo"

>> %timeit with_slots.foo
44.5 ns
>> %timeit without_slots.foo
54.5 ns
```

Even when you are simply trying to access with_slots.foo, it's much faster than accessing the attribute of the WithoutSlots class. In Python 3, __slots__ is 30 percent faster than without __slots__.

The second use case of __slots__ is for memory saving. __slots__ helps to reduce the space in memory that each object instance takes up. The space that __slots__ saves is significant.

You can find more information about __slots__ at https://docs. python.org/3/reference/datamodel.html#slots.

Another reason to use __slots__ is obviously to save space. If you consider Listing 4-8 and find out the size of object, then you can see that __slots__ saves space for objects compared to normal objects.

```
>> import sys
>> sys.getsizeof(with_slots)
48
>> sys.getsizeof(without_slots)
56
```

__slots__ helps you to save space for objects and gives you better performance compared to without __slots__ use. The question is, when should you consider using __slots__ in your code? To answer this question, let's briefly talk about instance creation.

When you create an instance of a class, extra space is automatically added to the instance to accommodate __dict__ and __weakrefs__. __dict__ is usually not initialized until you use it for attribute access, so you shouldn't worry about this much. However, when you create/access the attribute, then __slots__ makes much more sense compared to dict in cases where you need to save that extra space or make it performant.

However, whenever you don't want that extra space occupied by __dict__ in a class object, you can use __slots__ to save the space and for extra performance when you need to access attributes.

As an example, Listing 4-10 uses __slots__, and the child class doesn't create __dict__ for attribute a, which saves space and increases performance while accessing the a attribute.

Listing 4-10. __slots__ Faster Attribute Access

```
class Base:
    __slots__ = ()

class Child(Base):
    __slots__ = ('a',)

c = Child()
c.a = 'a'
```

The Python documentation recommends not using __slots__ for the majority of cases. In rare cases where you feel that you need that extra space and performance, give it a try.

I also recommend not using __slots__ until you really need that extra space and performance because it restricts you to using the class in a specific way, especially when dynamically assigning the variables. As an example, see Listing 4-11.

Listing 4-11. Attribute Error When Using __slots__

```
class User(object):
    __slots__ = ("first_name", )

>> user = User()
>> user.first_name = "Larry"
>> b.last_name = "Page"
AttributeError: "User" object has no attribute "last_name"
```

There are many ways to circumvent these issues, but those solutions won't help you much compared to using code without __slots__. As an example, if you want dynamic assignment, you can use the code shown in Listing 4-12.

Listing 4-12. Using __dict__ with __slots__ to Overcome the Dynamic Assignment Issue

```
class User:
    __slots__ = first_name, "__dict__"
>> user = User()
>> user.first_name = "Larry"
>> user.last_name = "Page"
```

So, with __dict__ in __slots__, you lose some of the size benefits, but the upside is that you get dynamic assignment.

The following are some other places where you should not use __slots__:

- When you are subclassing a built-in like a tuple or str and want to add attributes to it

- When you want to provide default values via class attributes for instance variables

So, consider using __slots__ when you really need that extra space and performance. It won't restrict you by limiting the class features and making debugging harder.

Change Class Behavior Using Metaclasses

Metaclasses help to customize the class behavior per your needs. Instead of creating some complex logic to add a specific behavior in a class, check out the Python metaclasses. They give you a nice tool to handle complex logic in your code. In this section, you will learn about using a magic method called __call__ to implement multiple features.

Let's say you want to prevent a client from directly creating the object of a class; you can easily achieve that using __call__. See Listing 4-13.

Listing 4-13. Prevent Creating an Object Directly

```
class NoClassInstance:
"""Create the user object."""
    def __call__(self, *args, **kwargs):
        raise TypeError("Can't instantiate directly""")

class User(metaclass=NoClassInstance):
    @staticmethod
    def print_name(name):
    """print name of the provided value."""
        print(f"Name: {name}")

>> user = User()
TypeError: Can't instantiate directly
>>> User.print_name("Larry Page")
Name: Larry Page
```

Here __call__ makes sure that the class is not being initiated directly from the client code; instead, it uses the static method.

Let's say you need to create an API where you want to apply a strategy design pattern or make it easier for client code to use your API.

Let's consider the example in Listing 4-14.

Listing 4-14. API Design Using __call__

```
class Calculation:
    """

    A wrapper around the different calculation algorithms that
    allows to perform different action on two numbers.
    """
```

```
    def __init__(self, operation):
        self.operation = operation

    def __call__(self, first_number, second_number):
        if isinstance(first_number, int) and isinstance(second_
        number, int):
            return self.operation()
        raise ValueError("Provide numbers")

def add(self, first, second):
    return first + second

def multiply(self, first, second):
    return first * second

>> add = Calculation(add)
>> print(add(5, 4))
9
>> multiply = Calculation(multiply)
>> print(multiply(5, 4))
20
```

Here you can send different methods or algorithms to perform specific actions without duplicating the common logic. Here you see code inside __call__, which makes your API much easier to use.

Let's look at one more scenario in Listing 4-15. Say you want to somehow create cached instances. When an object is being created with the same value, it caches the instance instead of creating a new instance for the same value, which could be really helpful when you don't want to duplicate an instance with the same parameters.

Listing 4-15. Implement Instance Caching Using __call__

```
class Memo(type):
    def __init__(self, *args, **kwargs):
        super().__init__(*args, **kwargs)
        self.__cache = {}

    def __call__(self, _id, *args, **kwargs):
        if _id not in self.__cache:
            self.cache[_id] = super().__call__(_id, *args, **kwargs)
        else:
            print("Existing Instance")
        return self.__cache[id]

class Foo(Memo):
    def __init__(self, _id, *args, **kwargs):
        self.id = _id

def test():
    first = Foo(id="first")
    second = Foo(id="first")
    print(id(first) == id(second))

>>> test()
True
```

I hope the __call__ use case helps you understand how metaclasses help you do some complicated tasks easily. __call__ also has some other nice use cases such as creating singletons, memorizing values, and using decorators.

Note   There are lots of other times where metaclasses can be used to achieve complicated tasks easily. I suggest digging into metaclasses and trying to understand the use cases of some of the metaclasses.

Learn About Python Descriptors

Python descriptors help to get, set, and delete attributes from an object's dictionary. When you access the class attribute, this starts the lookup chain. If the descriptor methods are defined in code, then the descriptor method will be invoked to look up the attributes. These descriptor methods are __get__, __set__, and __delete__ in Python.

In practical terms, when you assign or get a specific attribute value from a class instance, you might want to do some extra processing before setting the value of an attribute or while getting a value of the attributes. Python descriptors help you do those validation or extra operations without calling any specific method.

So, let's see an example that will help you understand a real use case, as shown in Listing 4-16.

Listing 4-16. Python Descriptor __get__ Example

```python
import random

class Dice:
"""Dice class to perform dice operations."""
    def __init__(self, sides=6):
        self.sides = sides

    def __get__(self, instance, owner):
        return int(random.random() * self.slides) + 1

    def __set__(self, instance, value):
        print(f"New assigned value: ${value}")
        if not isinstance(instance.sides, int):
            raise ValueError("Provide integer")
                instance.sides = value
```

```
class Play:
    d6 = Dice()
    d10 = Dice(10)
    d13 = Dice(13)

>> play = Play()
>>  play.d6
3
>>  play.d10
4
>> play.d6 = 11
New assigned value:  11

>> play.d6 = "11"
I am here with value:  11
-----------------------------------------------------------------
ValueError                                  Traceback (most
recent call last)
<ipython-input-66-47d52793a84d> in <module>()
----> 1 play.d6 = "11"

<ipython-input-59-97ab6dcfebae> in __set__(self, instance, value)
     9          print(f" New assigned value: {value}")
     10         if not isinstance(value, int):
---> 11             raise ValueError("Provide integer")
     12         self.sides = value
     13

ValueError: Provide integer
```

Here you are using the __get__ descriptor to provide extra functionality to a class attribute without calling any specific method, and you are using __set__ to make sure that you assign only int values to the Dice class attribute.

Let's briefly learn about these descriptors.

- `__get__(self, instance, owner)`: When you access the attribute, this method is automatically being called when defined, as shown in Listing 4-16

- `__set__(self, instance, owner)`: When you set the attribute of instance, this method is called as `obj.attr = "value"`.

- `__delete__(set, instance)`: When you want to delete a specific attribute, this descriptor is being called.

Descriptors give you more control over your code and can be used in different scenarios such as validating an attribute before assigning, making your attribute read-only, and so on. It also helps to make your code much cleaner because you don't need to create a specific method to do all these complicated validations or check operations.

Note   Descriptors are pretty useful when you want to set or get your class attributes in a cleaner way. If you understand how they work, it could be much more useful to you in other places where you want to perform specific attribute validation or checks. Ideally, this section helped give you a basic understanding of descriptors.

Summary

The metaclasses in Python are considered obscure because of their syntax and somewhat magic functionality. However, if you get a hold of some of the most used metaclasses discussed in this chapter, it will make your code better for an end user to use, and you will feel that you have better control over the way you shape your APIs or libraries for the user.

However, consider using them cautiously as sometimes using them to solve each problem in your code can impact the code's readability. Similarly, having a good understanding of modules in Python gives you a better idea of why and how to keep your modules following the SRP. I hope this chapter gave you enough insight into these two very important concepts in Python.

## CHAPTER 5

Decorators
and Context Managers

Decorators and context managers are an advanced topic in Python, but they are useful in many real-world scenarios. Many popular libraries use decorators and context managers extensively to make their APIs and code cleaner. Initially, it might be a little tricky to understand decorators and context managers, but once you master them, they can make your code cleaner.

In this chapter, you will learn about decorators and context managers. You will also explore when these features can be useful while writing your next Python project.

Note   Decorators and context managers are advanced concepts in Python. Under the hood they heavily use metaclasses. You don't need to learn about metaclasses to learn how to use decorators and context managers because Python gives you enough tools and libraries to create decorators and context managers without using any of the metaclasses. If you don't have much of an understanding of metaclasses, don't worry. You should be able to learn fully how decorators and context managers work. You will also learn some techniques to make it easier to write decorators and context

© Sunil Kapil 2019
S. Kapil, *Clean Python*, https://doi.org/10.1007/978-1-4842-4878-2_5

managers. I suggest getting a good grasp of both decorators and context manager concepts so you can recognize the places where you can use them in your code.

Decorators

Let's first talk about decorators. In this section, you will learn how decorators work and where in your real-world project you can use them. Decorators are an interesting and useful feature of Python. If you understand decorators well, you can build a lot of magical features without much effort.

Python decorators help you add behavior to functions or objects dynamically without changing the function or object behavior.

What Are Decorators, and Why Are They Useful?

Imagine you have several functions in your code and you need to add logging in all of them so that when they get executed, the function name gets logged in the log file or prints out on the console. One way to do that is to use a logging library and add a log line in each of these functions. It would take quite some time to do that, however, and it is also error prone because you are making lots of changes in the code to just add a log. Another way is to add the decorator on top of each function/class. This is much more effective and doesn't have the risk of adding new bugs to existing code.

In the Python world, decorators can be applied to functions, and they have the ability to run before and after the function they wrap. Decorators help to run additional code in functions. This allows you to access and modify input arguments and return values, which can be helpful in multiple places. Here are some examples:

- Rate limiting

- Caching values

- Timing the runtime of a function

- Logging purposes

- Caching exceptions or raising them

- Authentication

These are some of the main use cases for decorators; however, there are no limits to using them. In fact, you will find that API frameworks like flask heavily rely on decorators to turn functions into APIs. Listing 5-1 shows a flask example.

Listing 5-1. flask Example

```
from flask import Flask
app = Flask(__name__)

@app.route("/")
def hello():
    return "Hello World!"
```

This code turns the hello function into an API using the route decorator. This is the beauty of decorators, and having a good understanding of them will benefit you as developer because they can make your code cleaner and less error prone.

Understanding Decorators

In this section, you will see how to use decorators. Let's say you have a simple function that converts a passed-in string to uppercase and returns the result. See Listing 5-2.

Listing 5-2. Convert to Uppercase by Passing a String

```
def to_uppercase(text):
"""Convert text to uppercase and return to uppercase."""
    if not isinstance(text, str):
        raise TypeError("Not a string type")
    return text.upper()

>>> text = "Hello World"
>>> to_uppercase(text)
HELLO WORLD
```

This is a simple function that takes a string and converts it to uppercase. Let's make a small change in to_uppercase, as shown in Listing 5-3.

Listing 5-3. Convert to Uppercase by Passing func

```
def to_uppercase(func):
"""Convert to uppercase and return to uppercase."""

    # Adding this line, will call passed function to get text
    text = func()

    if not isinstance(text, str):
        raise TypeError("Not a string type")
    return text.upper()

def say():
    return "welcome"

def hello():
    return "hello"

>>> to_uppercase(say)
WELCOME

>>> to_uppercase(hello)
HELLO
```

Two changes were made.

- I modified the function to_uppercase to accept func instead of a string and call that function to get the string.

- I created a new function call that returns "welcome" and passed that function to the to_upper_case method.

The to_uppercase function calls the say function and gets text to convert to uppercase. So, to_uppercase gets the text by calling the function say instead of getting it from the passed argument.

Now, for the same code, you can write something like Listing 5-4.

Listing 5-4. Using Decorators

```
@to_uppercase
def say():
    return "welcome"

>>> say
WELCOME
```

Putting to_uppercase before a function as @to_uppercase makes the function to_uppercase a decorator function. This is similar to executing to_uppercase before the say function.

This is a simple example but is appropriate for showing how decorators work in Python. Now, the advantage of having to_uppercase as a decorator function is that you can apply it to any function to make the string uppercase. For example, see Listing 5-5.

Listing 5-5. Applying Decorators in Other Places

```
@to_uppercase
def say():
    return "welcome"

@to_uppercase
def hello():
    return "Hello"

@to_uppercase
def hi():
    return 'hi'

>>> say
WELCOME
>>> hello
HELLO
>>> hi
HI
```

This makes the code cleaner and easier to understand. Make sure that you make your decorator name explicit so that it's easy to understand what the decorator is trying to do.

Modify Behavior Using Decorators

Now that you know the fundamentals of decorators, let's go a little deeper to understand the main use case of decorators. In Listing 5-6, you will write a complex little function that wraps another function. So, you will modify the function to_uppercase to accept any function and then define another function under to_uppercase to perform the upper() operation.

Listing 5-6. Decorator for Uppercase

```
def to_uppercase(func):
    def wrapper():
        text = func()
        if not isinstance(text, str):
            raise TypeError("Not a string type")
        return text.upper()
    return wrapper
```

So, what's going here? You have a function call called to_uppercase where you pass func as a parameter like before, but here you move the rest of the code into another function called wrapper. The wrapper function is returned by to_uppercase.

The wrapper function allows you to execute the code here to change the behavior of the function instead of just running it. You can now do multiple things before the function executes and after the function completes the execution. The wrapper closure has access to the input function and can add new code before and after the function, which shows the actual power of the decorator function to change the behavior of the function.

The main use of having another function is to not execute the function until it's explicitly called. Until it's called, it will wrap the function and write the object of the function. So, you can write the full code as shown in Listing 5-7.

Listing 5-7. Full Code for Decorator for Uppercase

```
def to_uppercase(func):
    def wrapper():
        text = func()
        if not isinstance(text, str):
            raise TypeError("Not a string type")
        return text.upper()
    return wrapper
```

```
@to_uppercase
def say():
    return "welcome"

@to_uppercase
def hello():
    return "hello"

>>> say()
WELCOME
>>> hello()
HELLO
```

In above example, to_uppercase() is a define a decorator, which basically take any function as parameter and convert string to upper case. In above code say() function use to_uppercase as decorator, when python execute the function say(), python pass say() as a function object to to_uppercase() decorator at the execution time and return a function object called wrapper, which get executed when called as say() or hello().

You can utilize decorator almost all those scenario where you have to add functionality before running a specific function. Consider scenario, when you want your website users to login before seeing any page on your website, you can consider using login decorator on any function which allow user to access your website page, which will force users to login before see any page on your website. Similarity, consider a simple scenario where you want to add words "Larry Page" after the text, you can do that by adding the words as follows:

```
def to_uppercase(func):
    def wrapper():
        text = func()
        if not isinstance(text, str):
            raise TypeError("Not a string type")
```

```
        result = " ".join([text.upper(), "Larry Page"])
        return result
    return wrapper
```

Using Multiple Decorators

You can also apply multiple decorators to a function. Let's say you have to add a prefix before "Larry Page!" In that case, you can use a different decorator to add the prefix, as shown in Listing 5-8.

Listing 5-8. Multiple Decorators

```
def add_prefix(func):
    def wrapper():
        text = func()
        result " ".join([text, "Larry Page!"])
        return result
    return wrapper

 def to_uppercase(func):
    def wrapper():
        text = func()
        if not isinstance(text, str):
            raise TypeError("Not a string type")
        return text.upper()
    return wrapper

@to_uppercase
@add_prefix
def say():
    return "welcome"

>> say()
WELCOME LARRY PAGE!
```

As you might have already noticed, decorators get applied from bottom to top, so add_prefix is called first and then the to_uppercase decorator gets called. To prove this, if you change the order of decorators, you would get different results, as follows:

```
@add_prefix
@to_uppercase
def say():
    return "welcome"

>> say()
WELCOME Larry Page!
```

As you can notice, "Larry Page" doesn't get converted to uppercase because it was called last.

Decorators Accept Arguments

Let's expand on the previous example by passing arguments to decorator functions so you can dynamically change the passed arguments to uppercase and greet different people by name. See Listing 5-9.

Listing 5-9. Pass Arguments to Decorator Functions

```
def to_uppercase(func):
    def wrapper(*args, **kwargs):
        text = func(*args, **kwargs)
        if not isinstance(text, str):
            raise TypeError("Not a string type")
        return text.upper()
    return wrapper
```

```
@to_uppercase
def say(greet):
    return greet

>> say("hello, how you doing")
'HELLO, HOW YOU DOING'
```

As you can see, you can pass arguments to a decorator function, and it executes the code and uses those passed-in parameters in the decorator.

Consider Using a Library for Decorators

When you create a decorator, it mostly replaces one function with another function. Let's consider the simple example in Listing 5-10.

Listing 5-10. Decorator for Logging Function

```
def logging(func):
    def logs(*args, **kwargs):
        print(func.__name__ + " was called")
        return func(*args, **kwargs)
    return logs

@logging
def foo(x):
"""Calling function for logging"""
    return x * x

>>> fo = foo(10)
>>> print(foo.__name__)
logs
```

You might be expecting this to print foo as the function name. Instead, it prints logs as the function name, which is a wrapper function inside the decorator function logging. In fact, when you are using a decorator, you will always lose information such as __name__, __doc__, and so on.

To overcome this issue, you can consider using functool.wrap, which takes a function used in a decorator and adds the functionality of copying over the function name, docstring, arguments list, and so on. So, you can write the same code, as shown in Listing 5-11.

Listing 5-11. functools to Create Decorators

```
from functools import wraps
def logging(func):
    @wraps(func)
    def logs(*args, **kwargs):
        print(func.__name__ + " was called")
        return func(*args, **kwargs)
    return logs

@logging
def foo(x):
    """does some math"""
    return x + x * x

print(foo.__name__)  # prints 'f'
print(foo.__doc__)   # prints 'does some math'
```

The Python standard library has a library called functools that has funtools.wrap to create decorators that help to retain all the information, which otherwise could be lost when you create your own decorators.

Other than functools, there are libraries such as decorator, which is also really easy to use. Listing 5-12 shows an example.

Listing 5-12. Use a Decorator to Create a Decorator Function

```
from decorator import decorator

@decorator
def trace(f, *args, **kw):
    kwstr = ', '.join('%r: %r' % (k, kw[k]) for k in sorted(kw))
```

```
    print("calling %s with args %s, {%s}" % (f.__name__, args,
    kwstr))
    return f(*args, **kw)

@trace
def func(): pass

>>> func()
calling func with args (), {}
```

Similarly, you can use decorators inside the class for class methods, as shown in Listing 5-13.

Listing 5-13. Class Using a Function Decorator

```
def retry_requests(tries=3, delay=10):
    def try_request(fun):
        @wraps(fun)
        def retry_decorators(*args, *kwargs):
            for retry in retries:
                fun(*args, **kwargs)
                time.sleep(delay)
        return retry_decorators
    return try_request

class ApiRequest:
    def __init__(self, url, headers):
        self.url = url
        self.headers = headers

    @try_request(retries=4, delay=5)
    def make_request(self):
        try:
            response = requests.get(url, headers)
```

```
        if reponse.status_code in (500, 502, 503, 429):
            continue
    except Exception as error:
        raise FailedRequest("Not able to connect with server")
    return response
```

Class Decorators for Maintaining State and Validating Parameters

Until now, you have seen how to use functions as decorators, but Python doesn't have any restrictions on creating just methods as decorators. Classes can also be used as decorators. It all depends upon which specific way you want to define your decorators.

One of the main use cases of using class decorators is to maintain the state. However, let's first understand how the __call__ method helps your class to make it callable.

To make any class callable, Python provides special methods such as the __call__() method. What that means is that __call__ allows the class instance to be called as a function. Method like __call__ make it possible to create classes as decorators and return the class object to use as the function.

Let's look at the simple example in Listing 5-14 to further understand the __call__ method.

Listing 5-14. Use of the __call__ Method

```
class Count:
    def __init__(self, first=1):
        self.num = first

    def __call__(self):
        self.num += 1
        print(f"number of times called: {self.num}")
```

Now whenever you call the Count class using the instance to the class, the __call__ method will be called.

```
>>> count = Count()
>>> count()
Number to times called: 2

>>> count()
Number of times called: 3
```

As you can see, calling count() automatically calls the __call__ method, which maintains the state of the variable num.

You can use this concept to implement a decorator class. See Listing 5-15.

Listing 5-15. Maintain the State Using Decorators

```
class Count:
    def __init__(self, func):
        functools.update_wrapper(self, func)
        self.func = func
        self.num = 1

    def __call__(self, *args, *kwargs):
        self.num += 1
        print(f"Number of times called: {self.num}")
        return self.func(*args, *kwargs)

@Count
def counting_hello():
    print("Hello")

>>> counting_hello()
Number of times called: 2

>>> counting_hello()
Number of times called: 3
```

The __init__ method needs to store the reference of the function.
The __call__ method gets called whenever a function that decorates the
class gets called. The functools library is being used here to create the
decorator class. As you can see, you are storing the state of the variable
using class decorators.

Let's take a look at one more interesting case, as shown in Listing 5-16,
which could be achieved using class decorators, that is, type checking. This
is a simple example to showcase the use case; however, you can use it in all
kinds of cases where you need to check for a type of parameter.

Listing 5-16. Validate Parameters Using Class Decorators

```
class ValidateParameters:

    def __init__(self, func):
        functools.update(self, func)
        self.func = func

    def __call__(self, *parameters):
        if any([isinstance(item, int) for item in parameters]):
            raise TypeError("Parameter shouldn't be int!!")
        else:
            return self.func(*parameters)

@ValidateParameters
def add_numbers(*list_string):
    return "".join(list_string)

#  returns anb
print(concate("a", "n", "b"))

# raises Error.
print(concate("a", 1, "c"))
```

As you will notice, you are using class decorators to do type checking.

As you can see, there are a lot of places you can use decorators to make your code cleaner. Whenever you are considering using the decorator pattern, you can implement it using a Python decorator easily. Understanding decorators is a little tricky as it requires some level of understanding of how a function works, but once you get a basic understanding of decorators, consider using them in a real-world application. You will find that they make your code much cleaner.

Context Manager

Context managers, like decorators, are a useful feature of Python. You even might use them in your day-to-day code without realizing it, especially when you are using the Python built-in libraries. Common examples are file operations or socket operations.

Also, context managers can be really useful while writing APIs or third-party libraries because it makes your code much more readable and prevents client code from writing unnecessary code to clean up the resources.

Context Managers and Their Usefulness

As I mentioned, you probably unknowingly use context managers while doing different file or socket operations. See Listing 5-17.

Listing 5-17. File Operations Using a Context Manager

```
with open("temp.txt") as fread:
    for line in fread:
        print(f"Line: {line}")
```

Here the code is using a context manager to handle the operations. The with keyword is a way to use a context manager. To understand the usefulness of a context manager, let's write this code without a context manager, as shown in Listing 5-18.

Listing 5-18. File Operations Without a Context Manager

```
fread = open("temp.txt")
try:
    for line in fread:
        print(f"Line: {line}")
finally:
    fread.close()
```

The with statement was replaced by the try-finally block so that the client does not have to worry about handling exceptions.

The main usefulness of the context manager, besides a cleaner API, is resource management. Consider a scenario where you have a function that can read user input files, as shown in Listing 5-19.

Listing 5-19. Reading Files

```
def read_file(file_name):
"""Read given file and print lines."""
try:
    fread = open("temp.txt")
    for line in fread:
        print(f"Line: {line}")
catch IOError as error:
    print("Having issue while reading the file")
    raise
```

First, it's easy to forget to add the file.close() statement in the previous code. After reading the file, the file has not been closed by the read_file function. Now consider that the function read_file is being called thousands of times continuously; this would open thousands of file handlers in memory and might risk a memory leak. To prevent these cases, you can use a context manager, as shown in Listing 5-20.

Similarly, here you would have memory leak because the system has a limit on the number resources that can be used at a specific time. In the case of Listing 5-16, when you open a file, the OS assigns a resource called a *file descriptor*, which is limited by the OS. So, when that limit is passed, the program crashes with the message OSError.

Listing 5-20. Leak File Descriptor

```
fread = []
for x in range(900000):
    fread.append(open('testing.txt', 'w'))
```

```
>>> OSError: [Errno 24] Too many open files: testing.txt
```

Clearly, a context manager helps you to better handle resources. In this case, that includes closing the file and relinquishing the file descriptor once the file operation is done.

Understanding Context Managers

As you can see, context managers are useful for resource management. Let's see how you can build them.

To create a with statement, all you need to do is add the __enter__ and __exit__ methods to an object. Python will call these two methods when it needs to manage resources, so you don't need to worry about them.

So, let's look at the same example of opening a file and build a context manager . See Listing 5-21.

Listing 5-21. Managing Files

```
class ReadFile:
    def __init__ (self, name):
        self.name = name
    def __enter__ (self ):
        self . file = open (self.name, 'w' )
        return self
    def __exit__ (self,exc_type,exc_val,exc_tb):
        if self.file :
            self.file.close()

with ReadFile(file_name) as fread:
    f.write("Learning context manager")
    f.write("Writing into file")
```

Now when you run this code, as much as possible, you won't have a file descriptor leaking issue because ReadFile is managing that for you.

This works because when the with statement executes, Python calls the __enter__ function and executes. When execution leaves the context block (with), it executes __exit__ to free up the resources.

Let's look some of the rules of context managers.

- __enter__ returns an object that is assigned to the variable after as in a context manager block. This object usually is self.

- __exit__ calls the original context manager, not the one that is returned by __enter__.

- __exit__ won't be called if there is an exception or error in the __init__ or __enter__ method.

- Once the code block enters the context manager block, __enter__ will be called no matter what exception or error has been thrown.

- if __exit__ returns true, then any exception will be suppressed, and execution will exit from the context manager block without any error.

Let's try to understand these rules by looking at the example shown in Listing 5-22.

Listing 5-22. Context Manager Class

```
class ContextManager():
    def __init__(self):
        print("Crating Object")
        self.var = 0

    def __enter__(self):
        print("Inside __enter__")
        return self

    def __exit__(self, val_type, val, val_traceback):
        print('Inside __exit__')
        if exc_type:
            print(f"val_type: {val_type}")
            print(f"val: {val }")
            print(f"val_traceback: {val_traceback}")
>> context = ContextManager()
Creating Object
>> context.var
0
>> with ContextManager as cm:
>>     print("Inside the context manager")
```

159

```
Inside __enter__
Inside the context manager
Inside __exit__
```

Using contextlib to Build a Context Manager

Instead of writing classes to create a context manager, Python provides a library called a `contextlib.contextmanager` decorator. It is more convenient to write the context manager instead of writing classes.

The Python built-in library makes it easier to write a context manager. You don't need to write the whole class with all those __enter__ and __exit__ methods to create a context manager.

The `contextlib.contextmanager` decorator is a generator-based factory function for a resource that will automatically support the `with` statement, as shown in Listing 5-23.

Listing 5-23. Creating a Context Manager Using contextlib

```
from contextlib import contextmanager

@contextmanager
def write_file(file_name):
    try:
        fread = open(file_name, "w")
        yield fread
    finally:
        fread.close()

>> with read_file("accounts.txt") as f:
        f.write("Hello, how you are doing")
        f.write("Writing into file")
```

First, `write_file` acquires the resource, and then the `yield` keyword, which will be used by the caller, takes effect. When the caller exits from the with block, the generator continues to execute so that any remaining cleanup steps can occur such as cleaning up the resources.

When the @contextmanager decorator is used to create the context manager, the value that the generator yields is the context resource.

Both the class-based implementation and the contextlib decorator are similar implementations; it's a personal choice which you want to implement.

Some Practical Examples of Using a Context Manager

Let's look at where the context manager can be useful in day-to-day programming and in your projects.

There are many cases where you can use a context manager to make your code better, meaning without bugs and cleaner.

You will explore a couple of different scenarios where you can start using a context manager from day one. Besides these use cases, you can use a context manager in a lot of different feature implementations. For that, you need to find opportunities in your code that you think would be better when written using a context manager.

Accessing a Database

You can use a context manager while accessing database resources. When a specific process is working on some specific data in a database and modifying the value, you can lock the database while the process is working on that data, and once the operation is done, you can relinquish the lock.

As an example, Listing 5-24 shows some SQLite 3 code from https://docs.python.org/2/library/sqlite3.html#using-the-connection-as-a-context-manager

Listing 5-24. sqlite3 Lock

```
import sqlite3

con = sqlite3.connect(":memory:")
con.execute("create table person (id integer primary key,
firstname varchar unique)")

# Successful, con.commit() is called automatically afterwards
with con:
    con.execute("insert into person(firstname) values (?)",
    ("Joe",))

# con.rollback() is called after the with block finishes with
an exception, the
# exception is still raised and must be caught
try:
    with con:
        con.execute("insert into person(firstname) values (?)",
        ("Joe",))
except sqlite3.IntegrityError:
    print "couldn't add Joe twice"
```

Here you are using a context manager that automatically commits and rolls back in case of failure.

Writing Tests

While writing tests, a lot of time you want to mock specific services of tests with different kinds of exceptions thrown by code. In these cases, a context manager is really useful. Testing libraries like pytest have features that allow you to use a context manager to write the code that tests those exception or mock services. See Listing 5-25.

Listing 5-25. Testing Exception

```python
def divide_numbers(self, first, second):
    isinstance(first, int) and isintance(second, int):
        raise ValueError("Value should be int")

    try:
        return first/second
    except ZeroDevisionException:
        print("Value should not be zero")
        raise
with pytest.raises(ValueError):
    divide_numbers("1", 2)
```

You can also use it for mocking as:

```python
with mock.patch("new_class.method_name"):
    call_function()
```

mock.patch is an example of a context manager that can be used as a decorator.

Shared Resource

Using the with statement, you can allow access to only one process at a time. Assume you have to lock a file for writing in Python. It can be accessed from multiple Python processes at once, but you want only one process to be used at a time. You can do that using a context manager, as shown in Listing 5-26.

Listing 5-26. Lock File While Reading with Shared Resource

```
from filelock import FileLock

def write_file(file_name):
    with FileLock(file_name):
        # work with the file as it is now locked
        print("Lock acquired.")
```

This code is using the `filelock` library to lock the file so it's read by only one process.

A context manager block prevents you from entering another process to use the file while the operation is going on.

Remote Connection

In networking programming, you mostly interact with sockets and use a network protocol to access different things over the network. When you want to use a remote connection to access a resource or work on a remote connection, consider using a context manager to manage the resource. A remote connection is one of the best places to use a context manager. See Listing 5-27.

Listing 5-27. Lock File While Reading with Remote Connection

```
class Protocol:
    def __init__(self, host, port):
        self.host, self.port = host, port
    def __enter__(self):
        self._client = socket()
        self._client.connect((self.host, self.port))
        return self
    def __exit__(self, exception, value, traceback):
        self._client.close()
```

```
    def send(self, payload): <code for sending data>
    def receive(self): <code for receiving data>

with Protocol(host, port) as protocol:
    protocol.send(['get', signal])
    result = protocol.receive()
```

This code is using a context manager to access the remote connection using a socket. It takes care of a lot of things for you.

Note   A context manager can be used in a variety of cases. Start using context managers whenever you see an opportunity to manage resources or handle exceptions when writing tests. Context managers also make your API much cleaner and hide a lot of bottleneck code, which gives you a cleaner interface.

Summary

Decorators and context managers are first-class citizens in Python and should be your preference in your application design. Decorators are design patterns that allow you to add new functionality to an existing object without modifying the code. Similarly, a context manager allows you to manage your resources effectively. You can use them to run a specific piece of code before and after your function. They also help you to make your APIs cleaner and more readable. In the next chapter, you will explore some more tools such as generators and iterators to enhance the quality of your applications.

## CHAPTER 6

Generators and Iterators

Iterators and generators are useful tools in Python. They can make it easier to handle different data problems, and they help you to write code that is cleaner and performs better.

Python has a library to take advantage of these two features. You will learn about them in this chapter, and you will explore different problems that can be easily handled by generators and iterators without much effort.

Take Advantage of Iterators and Generators

In this section, you will explore different features of iterators and generators and will see where these two features can be used in your code to make it better. Both these features are useful mainly to solve different data problems.

Understanding Iterators

An *iterator* is an object that works on a stream of data. An iterator object has a method called __next__, and when you use a for loop, list comprehension, or anything that goes through all data points to get data

© Sunil Kapil 2019
S. Kapil, *Clean Python*, https://doi.org/10.1007/978-1-4842-4878-2_6

from an object or other data structure, in the background the __next__
method is being called.

Listing 6-1 shows how to create a class and make it an iterator.

Listing 6-1. Iterator Class

```
class MutiplyByTwo:
    def __init__(self, number):
        self.number = number
        self.count = 0

    def __next__(self):
        self.counter += 1
        return self.number * self.counter

mul = Mutiple(500)
print(next(mul))
print(next(mul))
print(next(mul))
>>> 500
>>> 1000
>>> 1500
```

Let's see how iterators actually work in Python. In the previous code,
you have a class called MultiplyByTwo that has a method called __next__
that returns a new iterator whenever it's called. The iterators need to keep
a record of where in is in the sequence by using a counter variable inside
__next__. However, if you try to use this class in a for loop, you will find
that it throws an error, as follows:

```
for num in MultiplyByTwo(500):
    print(num)
>>> MultiplyByTwo object is not iterable.
```

Interestingly, MultiplyByTwo is an iterator and not an iterable. So, the for loop won't work here. So, what's an iterable? Let's look at how iterables are different than iterators.

An iterable object has a method called __iter__, which returns an iterator. When __iter__ is called on any object, it returns the iterator, which can be used to iterate over the object to get the data. In Python, strings, lists, files, and dictionary are all examples of iterables.

When you try a for loop on them, it works nicely because the loop returns an iterator.

Now that you understand iterables vs. iterators, let's modify the class MultiplyByTwo to be an iterable. See Listing 6-2.

Listing 6-2. Iterator Class with the for Loop

```
class MultiplyByTwo:
    def __init__(self, num):
        self.num = num
        self.counter = 0

    def __iter__(self):
        return self

    def __next__(self):
        self.counter += 1
        return self.number * self.counter

for num in MutliplyByTwo(500):
    print(num)
```

This iterator runs forever, which might be useful in some cases, but what if you want to have a finite number of iterators? Listing 6-3 shows how you can implement this.

Listing 6-3. Iterator Class with StopIteration

```
class MultiplyByTwo:
    def __init__(self, num, limit):
        self.num = num
        self.limit = limit
        self.counter = 0

    def __iter__(self):
        return self

    def __next__(self):
        self.counter += 1
        value = self.number * self.counter

        if value > self.limit:
            raise StopIteration
        else:
          return value

for num in MutliplyByTwo(500, 5000):
    print(num)
```

When you raise StopIteration;, your MultiplyByTwo object gets the signal that it has exhausted the limit, raises an exception that is automatically handled by Python, and exits from the loop.

What Are Generators?

Generators are really useful for reading a large amount of data or a large number of files. Generators can be paused and resumed. Generators return objects that can iterate like lists. However, unlike lists, they are lazy and produce items one at a time. Generators are much more memory efficient when dealing with a large data set compared to any other data structure.

Let's try to create a similar multiply function as the iterator from the previous example. See Listing 6-4.

Listing 6-4. Generator Example

```
def multiple_generator(num, limit):
    counter = 1
    value = number * counter

    while value <= limit:
      yield value
      counter += 1
      value = number * counter

for num in multiple_generator(500, 5000):
    print(num)
```

You'll notice that this is way shorter than the iterator example, as you don't need to define __next__ and __iter__. You also don't need to keep track of internal state or raise an exception.

The new thing that you might have noticed is the yield keyword. yield is similar to return, but instead of terminating the function, it simply pauses execution until asking for another value. Generators are much more readable and performant compared to iterators.

When to Use Iterators

Iterators are really useful when you are dealing with a large set of numbers in the form of files or streams of data. Iterators give you the flexibility to handle the data one piece at a time instead of loading all the data in memory.

Let's assume you have a CSV file with a sequence of numbers and you need to calculate the sum of numbers from this CSV file. You can do this either by storing the sequence of data from the CSV file in a list and then

171

calculating the sum or by using an iterator approach where you read the CSV file row by row and calculate the sum of each row.

Let's look at both ways so you can understand the difference, as shown in Listing 6-5.

Listing 6-5. Read a CSV File Using a List

```
import csv
data = []
sum_data = 0
with open("numbers.csv", "r") as f:
  data.extend(list(csv.reader(f)))
for row in data[1:]:
  sum_data += sum(map(int, row))
print(sum_data)
```

Notice that you are saving data in a list here and then calculating the sum of numbers from the list. This can be more costly in terms of memory and can lead to a memory leak because you are duplicating the data in memory in the form of a CSV file and list, which could be dangerous if you are reading a large file. Here, an iterator can save you by getting only one row from the CSV file, so you are not dumping all the data in memory at one time. See Listing 6-6.

Listing 6-6. Read a CSV File Using an Iterator

```
import csv
sum_data = 0
with open('numbers.csv', 'r') as f:
  reader = csv.reader(f)
  for row in list(reader)[1:]:
      sum_data += sum(map(int, row))
print(sum_data)
```

This code is calculating the sum of one row and adding it to the next row by asking the iterator to give you a new set of data from a CSV file.

Another use case for an iterator is when you are reading data from a database. Let's consider a scenario where an e-commerce company sells products through an online store and users buy those products through an online payment. The payments of users are stored in a table called Payment, and after 24 hours, an automated system queries the Payment table and calculates the total profit made in the last 24 hours.

There are two approaches to solving this problem. The first option is to query the Payment table and get a list of amounts and then calculate the sum of those amounts. On a normal day, this might work, but consider a specific day such as Black Friday or a holiday when a company has millions of transactions. It could crash the system to load millions of records in memory at one time. The second option is to query the table but get the data by row or by a number of rows like 100 or 1,000 and then calculate the total transaction. In Django, you can do something like the code shown in Listing 6-7.

Listing 6-7. Read Payment Information from a Database Using an Iterator

```
def get_total_payment():
    payments = Payment.objects.all()
    sum_amount = 0
    if payments.exists():
        for payment in payments.iterator():
            sum_amount += payment
    return sum_amount
```

This code is calculating the total amount by fetching the data from a database one row at a time without loading all the data at once.

Using itertools

Python has a module called `itertools` that has collections of useful methods. I can't cover all the methods here but will talk about some of them.

combinations()

`itertools.combinations(iterable, r)`

This tool gives the combination tuples of `iterable` that are `r` length, which is 2 in the previous line.

```
from itertools import combinations

print(list(combinations('12345',2)))
[('1', '2'), ('1', '3'), ('1', '4'), ('1', '5'),
 ('2', '3'), ('2', '4'), ('2', '5'),
 ('3', '4'), ('3', '5'),
 ('4', '5')
]
```

permuations()

`itertools.permutations(iterable, r)`

This returns all the permutations of r length; if r is None, then the default length of r is the length of an iterable.

```
from itertools import permutations

print(permutations(['1','2','3']))

print(list(permutations(['1','2','3'])))
[('1', '2', '3'), ('1', '3', '2'),
 ('2', '1', '3'), ('2', '3', '1'),
 ('3', '1', '2'), ('3', '2', '1')
]
```

product()

```
itertools.product(iterable, r)
```

This tool computes the Cartesian product of the input iterable. It's similar to a nested loop.

As an example, product(x, y) would look as follows:

```
((x,y) for x in A for y in B)
```

```
from itertools import product
```

```
print(list(product([1,2,3],repeat = 2)))
[(1, 1), (1, 2), (1, 3),
 (2, 1), (2, 2), (2, 3),
 (3, 1), (3, 2), (3, 3)
]
```

count()

```
itertools.count(start=0, step=1)
```

count() is an iterator that returns with numbers evenly spaced beginning with the number start.

As an example, you tell count() to return a number iterator with step 4.

```
import itertools
```

```
for num in itertools.count(1, 4):
    print(item)
    if item > 24:
        break
```

```
>>> 1, 5, 9, 13, 17, 21
```

groupby()

```
itertools.groupby(iterable, key=None)
```

```
itertools.groupby tool helps you to group items.
```

As a simple example, let's say you need to group characters as follows:

```
numbers = 555441222
result = []
for num, length in groupby(numbers):
    result.append((len(list(length)), int(num)))
```

```
print(*result)
```

```
>>> (3, 5)(2,4)(1,1)(3,2)
```

There are other useful methods in itertools that are really useful.
I suggest you check out https://docs.python.org/3.7/library/
itertools.html for more information.

Why Generators Are Useful

Like iterators, generators save memory. Because iterators are capable of
doing lazy evolution, you can save memory by getting only the data an
operation needs. Therefore, you can use generators when reading big files
from a database to save memory and CPU cycles.

So, let's say you want to read the file the lazy way; you can use the
yield keyword, which creates a generator function for you. See Listing 6-8.

Listing 6-8. Read in a Chunk Using a Generator

```
def read_in_chunks(file_handler, chunk_size=1024):
    """Lazy function (generator) to read a file piece by piece.
    Default chunk size: 1k."""
    while True:
```

```
        data = file_handler.read(chunk_size)
        if not data:
            break
        yield data

f = open('large_number_of_data.dat')
for piece in read_in_chunks(f):
    print(piece)
```

Here you are reading a big file in a chunk instead of loading the while file in memory.

List Comprehension vs. Iterators

List comprehension and iterators are two different ways to generate numbers, and they have a significant difference in terms of how they save the data in memory or perform operations while generating numbers.

```
# This is iterators expression to generate numbers up to 200.
 (x*2 for x in xrange(200))
# List comprehension expression to generate numbers up to 200

  [x*2 for x in xrange(200)]
```

The main difference here is that list comprehension saves all 200 numbers in memory once it completes. However, iterators create an iterable object that generates numbers on the fly, so speed is fast in the iterator case. Also, an iterator gives you the flexibility to pass around objects to generate a number on the fly.

Take Advantage of the yield Keyword

Before digging into yield, I'll talk about how to work with the yield keyword in Python.

When you define yield inside one of your functions, calling the function gives you a generator object; however, that doesn't run your function. Once you get a generator object and each time you extract an object from the generator (either by using a for loop or by using next()), Python will execute the function until it comes to the yield keyword. Once Python reaches the yield keyword, it delivers the object and pauses until you extract it. Once you extract the object, Python resumes and runs the code after yield, continuing until it reaches another yield (which could be the same yield keyword or a different yield). Once a generator is exhausted, it will exit with a StopIteration exception, which the for loop automatically handles.

In other words, yield is a keyword that is used like return, except the function returns a generator. See Listing 6-9.

Listing 6-9. Generate a Number Using a Generator

```python
def generate_numbers(limit):
    for item in xrange(limit):
        yield item*item
        print(f"Inside the yield: {item}")

numbers = generate_numbers() # create a generator

print(numbers) # numbers is an object!
<generator object generate_numbers at 0xb7555c34>

for item in numbers:
    print(item)
0
1
4
```

Here you created a generator function using the yield keyword. Notice that when you call the function generate_numbers(), you get the numbers object, which is a generator object. You can then use this to generate numbers on the fly.

When you first call the generator object in a `for` loop, it runs the function from the start of `generator_numbers` until it encounters the `yield` keyword, and then it stops and returns the first value of the loop. Once it calls a second time, it starts on the next line, which is `print(f"Inside the yield: {item}")`. It continues to do that until it reaches a limit.

yield from

The `yield from` keyword has been used since Python 3. The main use case of `yield from` is to get a value from other generators, as shown in Listing 6-10.

Listing 6-10. Generate a Number Using the yield from Keyword

```
def flat_list(iter_values):
    """flatten a multi list or something."""
    for item in iter_values:
        if hasattr(item, '__iter__'):
            yield from flat_list(item)
        else:
            yield item

print(list(flat_list([1, [2], [3, [4]]])))
>>> [1, 2, 3, 4]
```

Instead of iterating over `flat_list`, you are using `yield from`, which not only shorten the lines but also makes your code cleaner.

yield Is Faster Compared to a Data Structure

If you are dealing with a lot of data and need speed, then obviously you should use generators to generate the data instead of relying on a data structure like a list or a tuple.

Here is a simple example:

```
data = range(1000)
def using_yield():
    def wrapper():
        for d in data:
            yield d
    return list(wrapper())

def using_list():
    result = []
    for d in data:
        result.append(d)
    return result
```

If you run both code examples, you will notice that using yield is definitely faster than using a list.

Summary

Generators and iterators are really useful, especially when you are dealing with a lot of data or big files. You need to be extra cautious about memory and CPU consumption as over consumption ould lead to issues such as memory leaks. Python gives you tools like itertools and yield to help you avoid all these issues. Be extra diligent when you are dealing with large files, working with databases, or calling multiple APIs; you might be able to use these tools to make your code cleaner and performant.

CHAPTER 7

Utilize New Python Features

The new features introduced in the latest Python 3 version have made
Python much more fun to write programs in. Python already had a lot
of great features, and Python 3 has made it a much more feature-rich
language. Python 3 comes with features such as native support for async
programming, typing, better performance, iterator improvements, and
so on.

In this chapter, you will learn about the new features that can make
your code better and more performant compared to previous versions
of Python. You will learn how using any or all of these features could be
useful and where should you consider using them in your code.

Note   You can explore the new features of Python in the
official documentation at `https://docs.python.org/3/`
`whatsnew/3.7.html`. Python 3 is still in development at the time
of writing this book, so there might be some improvements not
mentioned here. In other words, keep an eye on the Python official
documentation for the most up-to-date features.

© Sunil Kapil 2019
S. Kapil, *Clean Python*, https://doi.org/10.1007/978-1-4842-4878-2_7

Asynchronous Programming

If you have ever done any asynchronous programming (or *async programming* for short) in another language like JavaScript, you might know that it's not an easy topic. Before Python 3.4, there was a way to do async programming using third-party libraries, but it always felt a bit clumsy compared to a language like NodeJS, which is very friendly to async programming.

Python is flexible on the matter because you can write both sync and async code. Using async programming can make your code much more efficient and performant compared to sync programming because it uses the resources more effectively. However, it's really important to know when you should use async programming and when you shouldn't.

Before going further, let's discuss asynchronous versus synchronous programming. In the synchronous world, things happen one at a time. You call a function or operation, and your program control waits for it to complete before it proceeds to do the next thing. When a function finishes its operation, the function returns the result. While the operation is being performed by the function, your system doesn't do anything else besides wait for it to finish.

In the asynchronous world, multiple things can happen at the same time. When you start an action or call a function, your program continues to run, and you can perform other actions or call other functions instead of just waiting for that async function to finish. Once the async function has completed the work, the program control can access the result.

As an example, let's assume you have to get stock data for different companies by calling different companies' stock APIs. In synchronous code, you would call the first stock API and wait to get the reply, and then you would make another call and wait for it to complete. This is a simple way to run a program; however, the program spends too much time waiting for responses. In async code, you call the first stock API, then the second, and the third, and you continue until you get results from one of those APIs. You collect the results and continue calling other stock APIs instead of waiting for the results.

In this section, you will explore async programming in Python so you can understand how to use it. These are the three main building blocks of Python async programming:

- The main task of the *event loop* is to manage different tasks and distribute them for execution. The event loop registers each task and takes care of the flow control between these tasks.

- *Coroutines* are functions that schedule an event loop to run. An `await` releases the flow of control back to the event loop.

- *Futures* represent the result of a task that may or may not have been executed. This result may be an exception.

Introducing async in Python

To achieve async paradigm in Python programming, Python has introduced two main components.

- **asyncio**: This is the Python package that allows an API to run and manage coroutines.

- **async/await**: Python has introduced two new keywords to work with async code. They help you to define coroutines.

Basically, Python now has the capability to run in two different ways, either asynchronously or synchronously. Depending on which way you choose, you should think differently when you design your code because the functionality and behavior of code is different. These styles also have different libraries from each other. In other words, both the style and the syntax of asynchronous and synchronous coding are different from each other.

To illustrate this point, if you are making HTTP calls, you can't use the blocking `requests` library; therefore, you might want to consider using `aiohttp` to make HTTP calls. Similarly, if you are working with the Mongo driver, you can't rely on synchronous drivers like `mongo-python`. You have to use an asynchronous driver like `motor` to access MongoDB.

In the synchronous world, there is no easy way to achieve concurrency or parallelism in Python. However, there are options to run code in parallel using the thread model of Python; however, in the asynchronous world (don't confuse this with parallelism), things have changed for the better. Now everything runs in an event loop, which lets you run several coroutines at once. These coroutines run synchronously until they hit `await` and then they pause, giving control to the event loop. The other coroutine will have a chance to perform an action, or some other thing will happen.

It's also important to note that you can't mix async and sync code in the same function. As an example, you can't use `await` with a sync function.

There are couple of things you should be aware of before diving into asynchronous programming, especially in the Python world.

- In synchronous programming, when you want to halt the execution or make a program not do anything, you usually use the Python `time.sleep(10)` function. However, in the asynchronous world, this won't work as you expect. You should be using `await asyncio.sleep(10)`; this doesn't return control to the event loop, and it can hold up the entire process. Nothing else will happen, which might be a good thing considering this makes it harder for a race condition to happen when code is moving from one `await` call to another.

- If you use blocking code in an asynchronous function, Python won't complain about you using it; however, things will slow down painfully. Also, Python has debug mode, which will warn you about things that are blocking for too long with common errors.

- You might need to consider having duplicate code when you are writing asynchronous and synchronous code in the same codebase. It might not be possible in most of the cases that you use the same library or helper for both async and sync code.

- While writing asynchronous code, you should assume that the control flow at the time of execution might be lost as compared to the full control of synchronous code. Especially when you have multiple coroutines that are running in your code, multiple things are happening.

- As you can imagine, debugging gets harder in the asynchronous world. There are no good tools or techniques as of now for debugging.

- Testing async code is not very convenient in Python. There is a lack of good libraries to test async code. You might see some libraries that are trying to achieve this, but they are not that mature as in some other programming languages like JavaScript.

- Using `async` keywords of Python in synchronous code like `await` inside a synchronous function will give you a syntax error.

It's also important to change your mind-set about designing your code asynchronously. If you have both async and sync code in your codebase, then you have to see them differently. Anything inside async def is async code, and everything else is synchronous code.

There are two cases when you should consider using async code.

- Calling async code from async code, you can use all the Python keywords like await and async to fully utilize Python async coding.

- Calling async code from sync code is now possible with Python 3.7 by just calling the run() function in asyncio.

Overall, writing async code is not as easy as writing synchronous code in Python. The Python async model is based on concepts such as events, callbacks, transports, protocols, and futures. The good news is that the asyncio library is evolving, and each release is being improved. Python asyncio is here to stay!

Note   Before writing any async code, make sure you get in the right mind-set about writing the code in an async way, especially when you have a synchronous programming background. There will be lots of times you feel like you can't figure async programming out. Using async code in small bits and introducing it into your codebase with minimal impact is a good way to start using it. Having good tests for async code will make sure that the changes in your codebase don't break existing functionality. Things are moving fast in the async world of Python for the better. So, keep an eye on the new release of Python for all the new features in async programming.

How It Works

I have talked about some of the background of asyncio features, so let's now see how asyncio works in the real world. Python introduced the asyncio package to write async code. The package provides two keys, async and await. Let's dive into a simple async example to see how Python async actually works. See Listing 7-1.

Listing 7-1. Async, Simple Hello Example

```python
import asyncio

async def hello(first_print, second_print):
    print(first_print)
    await asyncio.sleep(1)
    print(second_print)

asyncio.run(hello("Welcome", "Good-bye"))
Welcome
Good-bye
```

Listing 7-1 shows some simple asyncio code; it first prints Welcome and then after one second prints Good-bye. Let's see how this works. First asyncio.run() calls the async function hello with two parameters passed in: Welcome and Good-bye. When the hello function is called, it first prints first_print and then waits for one second to print second_print. This behavior might look like synchronous code; however, getting into the details might surprise you and will help you to understand how the asynchronous code actually works. Let's first understand some of the terms being used here.

Coroutine Function

Any function that is defined as `async def` can be called a *coroutine* in Python. Here, `async def hello(first_print, second_print)` could be called a coroutine function.

Coroutine Object

The object returned by calling a coroutine function is called a *coroutine object*. You will see examples later where it might be clearer what the difference is between a coroutine function and a coroutine object in the real world.

asyncio.run()

This function is part of the `asyncio` module. This is the main entry point for any async code and should be called only once. It does a couple of things.

- It has responsibility to run the passed coroutine, which is running the `async def hello` coroutine function in the previous example.

- It also manages the `asyncio` event loop. This basically creates a new event loop and closes it at the end.

await

`await` is a keyword that passes function control back to the event loop and suspends the execution of the coroutine. In the previous example, when Python encounters the `await` keyword, it suspends the `hello` coroutine execution for one second and passes control back to the event loop, which resumes after one second.

Before going into detail, let's look at one more simple example and see what happens. `await` usually suspends execution of a coroutine function until whatever it's waiting for. When the result of the coroutine is returned, the execution resumes. There are some rules for await.

- It can be used only inside the async def function.

- If you define it in a normal function, it will raise an exception.

- To call a coroutine function, you must wait for the results to come back.

- When you use something like await func(), it's required that func() be an object that is awaitable, which means it should be either another coroutine function or an object that defined an __await__() method that returns an iterator.

Let's now see a more useful example, as shown in Listing 7-2, where you will try to run things concurrently and utilize the async feature.

Listing 7-2. asyncio Running Two Tasks

```
import asyncio
import time

async def say_something(delay, words):
    print(f"Before: {words}")
    await asyncio.sleep(delay)
    print(f"After: {words}")

async def main():
    print(f"start: {time.strftime('%X')}")

    await say_something(1, "First task started.")
    await say_something(1, "Second task started.")

    print(f"Finished: {time.strftime('%X')}")

asyncio.run(main())
```

Here is the result:

```
start: 11:30:11
Before: First task started.
After: First task started.
Before: Second task started.
After: Second task started.
Finished: 11:30:13
```

Here, you are running the same coroutine two times by calling the coroutine function say_something two times and waiting for both versions to finish. As you will notice in the result, the say_something coroutine runs first and waits for one second and then finishes the coroutine. Then it is called again by the main() coroutine to perform another task, which is to print a second task after one second. This is not what you want when using async; it still looks like synchronous code is running. The main idea behind async code is that you can run say_something two times concurrently.

Let's convert this code and run it concurrently, as shown in Listing 7-3. You might notice some significant changes in the code compared to the previous listing.

Listing 7-3. asyncio Running Code Concurrently

```python
import asyncio
import time

async def say_something(delay, words):
    print(f"Before: {words}")
    await asyncio.sleep(delay)
    print(f"After: {words}")
```

```python
async def main():
    print(f"Starting Tasks: {time.strftime('%X')}")
    task1 = asyncio.create_task(say_something(1, "First task
    started"))
    task2 = asyncio.create_task(say_something(2, "Second task
    started"))

    await task1
    await task2

    print(f"Finished Tasks: {time.strftime('%X')}")

asyncio.run(main())
```

Here is the result:

```
Starting Tasks: 11:43:56
Before: First task started
Before: Second task started
After: First task started
After: Second task started
Finished Tasks: 11:43:58
```

As you can see in the result, this function is running the same coroutines with different parameters concurrently, which is what you wanted to do to run things concurrently.

Let's analyze what happened in this example:

- The say_something coroutine starts with the parameter's first task, called task1.

- It then suspends the execution for one second as it encounters the await keyword.

- Once await is encountered by task1, it suspends the running coroutine and returns the control to the event loop.

- Another task called task2 is created by wrapping the coroutine's function say_something inside create_task with parameters.

- When the second task, task2, starts running, it encounters the await keyword similar to task1 in the async def say_something coroutine.

- Then it makes task2 suspend for two seconds and returns control to the event loop.

- Now the event loop resumes the first task (task1) because asyncio.sleep has finished (which is sleeping for one second).

- When task task1 completes the work, the second task, task2, resumes the task and finishes it.

The first thing you might have noticed here is asyncio.create_task(), which makes the function run the coroutine concurrently as an asyncio task.

Tasks

Whenever any coroutine function is called using a method like asyncio.create_task(), that coroutine is automatically scheduled to run soon.

Tasks help you to run your coroutine functions concurrently, and Python calls those running coroutines *tasks* in the Python asyncio world. Let's look at a simple example of creating a task using the asyncio library; see Listing 7-4.

Listing 7-4. Simple Task Creation Example

```
import asyncio

async def value(val):
    return val
```

```python
async def main():
    # Creating a task to run concurrently
    # You can create as many task as possible here
    task = asyncio.create_task(value(89))

    # This will simply wait for task to finish
    await task

asyncio.run(main())
```

Another way to create tasks and wait for all of them to complete is to
use the asyncio.gather function. asyncio.gather has the capability to
run all the coroutine functions as tasks and wait for their results before
returning to the event loop.

Let's look at a simple example; see Listing 7-5.

Listing 7-5. Using asyncio.gather to Run Tasks Concurrently

```python
import asyncio
import time

async def greetings():
    print("Welcome")
    await asyncio.sleep(1)
    print("Good By")

async def main():
    await asyncio.gather(greetings(), greetings())

def say_greet():
    start = time.perf_counter()
    asyncio.run(main())
    elapsed = time.perf_counter() - start
    print(f"Total time elapsed: {elapsed}")

asyncio.run(say_greet())
```

When you run this code, you will see something like this:

```
Welcome
Welcome
Good By
Good By
Total time elapsed: 1.006283138
```

Let's try to understand how the previous code is running using `asyncio.gather`. When you run this code, you will notice that `Welcome` appears on the console two times and then `Good By` runs two times. There is slight delay between printing two `Welcome` and two `Good By` messages.

When you call the async `main()` function from `say_greet()`, then it's the event loop's job to talk to the `greetings()` function, and executing `greetings()` can be called a *task*.

In the previous code, you have two tasks running that can execute the `greetings()` function.

One of the topics that I haven't talked about is the `await` keyword. This is one of the important keywords in `asyncio` programming in Python. Any object that you can use with `await` can be called an *awaitable* object. It's also important to have an understanding of awaitable objects because it will give you a better picture of how the `asyncio` library operates and how to switch between different tasks in Python.

Awaitable Objects

As already mentioned, any object that you use with `await` is called an awaitable object. Most of the `asyncio` APIs accept awaitable objects.

Awaitable objects have the following types in asynchronous code.

Coroutines

I already touched on the concept of coroutines in the previous section. Here you will further explore this and see how it's one of the awaitable types.

All coroutine functions are awaitable, so they can be awaited from other coroutines. You can also define a coroutine as a subroutine, but it can exit without destroying the state in the async world. See Listing 7-6.

Listing 7-6. Coroutine Awaiting from Another Coroutine

```python
import asyncio

async def mult(first, second):
    print(f"Calculating multiply of {first} and {second}")
    await asyncio.sleep(1)
    num_mul = first * second
    print(f"Multiply of {num_mul}")
    return num_mul

async def sum(first, second):
    print(f"Calculating sum of {first} and {second}")
    await asyncio.sleep(1)
    num_sum = first + second
    print(f"Sum is {num_sum}")
    return num_sum

async def main(first, second):
    await sum(first, second)
    await mult(first, second)

asyncio.run(main(7, 8))
```

Here is the result:

```
Calculating sum of 7 and 8
Sum is 15
Calculating multiply of 7 and 8
Multiply of 56
```

As you will notice in the example, you are calling coroutines multiple times and using a coroutine with the await keyword.

Tasks

The coroutine is scheduled to run when it is wrapped in a task using the asyncio.create_task() method of asyncio. Most of the time, if you are working with async code, you are dealing with the create_task method to run your coroutine concurrently. See Listing 7-7.

Listing 7-7. create_task Helping to Schedule a Coroutine to Run

```python
import asyncio

async def mul(first, second):
    print(f"Calculating multiply of {first} and {second}")
    await asyncio.sleep(1)
    num_mul = first * second
    print(f"Multiply of {num_mul}")
    return num_mul

async def sum(first, second):
    print(f"Calculating sum of {first} and {second}")
    await asyncio.sleep(1)
    num_sum = first + second
    print(f"Sum is {num_sum}")
    return num_sum

async def main(first, second):
    sum_task = asyncio.create_task(sum(first, second))
    mul_task = asyncio.create_task(sum(first, second))
    await sum_task
    await mul_task

asyncio.run(main(7, 8))
```

Here is the result:

```
Calculating sum of 7 and 8
Calculating sum of 7 and 8
Sum is 15
Sum is 15
```

As you can see in this example, you are running two different coroutines concurrently by leveraging the `asyncio` method `asyncio.create_task` for creating tasks.

Once a task has been created, you use the `await` keyword to run the newly created task concurrently. Once both tasks are completed, you send the result to an event loop.

Futures

Futures are awaitable objects that represent a future result of an asynchronous operation. A coroutine needs to wait until the `Future` object returns the response or completes the operation. Mostly, you won't be using a `Future` object explicitly in your code. However, the `Future` object has been implicitly taken care of by `asyncio`.

When a future instance is being created, that means it's not completed yet but will be some time later in the future.

`Future` has methods like `done()` and `cancel()`. You mostly don't need to write code like this, though, but having an understanding of the `Future` object is essential.

`Future` objects implement the `__await__()` method, and the job of the `Future` object is to hold a certain state and result.

`Future` has the following statuses:

- `PENDING`: This specifies that a `Future` is waiting to complete.

- `CANCELLED`: As mentioned, a `Future` object can be canceled using the cancel method.

197

- FINISHED: There are two ways a Future object can be completed: as Future.set_result() or as an exception with Future.set_exception().

Listing 7-8 shows an example of a Future object.

Listing 7-8. Future Object

```
from asyncio import Future

future = Future()
future.done()
```

Here is the result:

```
False
```

It might be a good time to learn more about asyncio.gather, as you might now have better understanding of how awaitable methods work in the asyncio world.

Note   Here I cover only the gather method; however, I advise you to look at other asyncio methods as well to see what their syntax looks like. Mostly, you will get an idea of which kind of input these functions require and why.

Its syntax looks like this:

```
asyncio.gather(*aws, loop=None, return_exceptions=False)
```

aws could be one coroutine or a list of coroutines that are scheduled to a task. When all the tasks are completed, the asyncio.gather method aggregates them and returns the result. It runs the task as per the order of those awaitable objects.

By default, the value of return_exceptions is False, which means if any of the tasks return exceptions, other tasks that are running currently won't be halted and will continue to run.

If the value of return_exception is True, it will be considered a successful result and will be aggregated in the result list.

Timeouts

Beside of raising an exception, you can do some kind of timeout when you are waiting for tasks to complete.

asyncio has a method called asyncio.wait_for(aws, timeout, *) that you can use to set a timeout for the task to run. If a timeout occurs, it cancels the task and raises the exception as asyncio.TimeoutError. The timeout value can be None or float or int; if the timeout is None, it blocks until the Future object is completed.

Listing 7-9 shows an example of an async timeout.

Listing 7-9. Async Timeout

```
import asyncio

async def long_time_taking_method():
    await asyncio.sleep(4000)
    print("Completed the work")

async def main():
    try:
        await asyncio.wait_for(long_time_taking_method(),
        timeout=2)
    except asyncio.TimeoutError:
        print("Timeout occurred")

asyncio.run(main())

    >> Timeout occurred
```

In Listing 7-9, the method `long_time_taking_method` takes around 4,000 seconds; however, you have set the timeout for the `Future` object to two seconds, so it goes to `asyncio.TimeoutError` after two seconds if the results are not available.

Note   The methods discussed in this section are the most common in `asyncio` code; however, there are couple other libraries and methods that are present in the `asyncio` library that are less common or for more advanced scenarios. You can take a look the Python official documentation if you are interested in learning more about `asyncio`.

Async Generators

Async generators make it possible to use `yield` in the `async` function. So, any `async` function that contains `yield` can be called an async generator. The idea of having an async generator is to replicate what the synchronous `yield` does. The only difference is that you can call that function as `async`.

Async generators certainly improve the performance of generators compared to the synchronous `yield`. As per the Python documentation, asynchronous generators are 2.3 times faster than synchronous generators. See Listing 7-10.

Listing 7-10. Async Generators

```
import asyncio

async def generator(limit):
    for item in range(limit):
        yield item
        await asyncio.sleep(1)
```

```
async def main():
    async for item in generator(10):
        print(item)

asyncio.run(main())
```

This will print items 1 to 9 within a one-second difference . This example shows how you can use async generators in your code within async coroutines.

Async Comprehensions

The Python async functionality provides a facility to implement async comprehension similar to the way synchronous code has comprehension for list, dict, tuple, and set. In other words, async comprehension is similar to using comprehension in async code.

Let's look at the example in Listing 7-11, which shows how you can utilize async comprehension.

Listing 7-11. Async Comprehension

```
import asyncio

async def gen_power_two(limit):
    item = 0
    while item < limit:
        yield 2 ** item
        item += 1
        await asyncio.sleep(1)

async def main(limit):
    gen = [item async for item in gen_power_two(limit)]
    return gen

print(asyncio.run(main(5)))
```

This will print a list of numbers from 2 to 16; however, you have to wait for five seconds to see the results as it will complete all the tasks and then return the result.

Async Iterators

You have already seen some examples of iterators such as `asyncio.gather`, which is one form of iterator.

In Listing 7-12, you can take a look at an iterator using `asyncio.as_completed()`, which gets tasks as they complete.

Listing 7-12. async Iterator Using as_completed

```python
import asyncio

async def is_odd(data):
    odd_even = []
    for item in data:
        odd_even.append((item, "Even") if item % 2 == 0 else
        (item, "Odd"))
    await asyncio.sleep(1)
    return odd_even

async def is_prime(data):
    primes = []
    for item in data:
        if item <= 1:
            primes.append((item, "Not Prime"))
        if item <= 3:
            primes.append((item, "Prime"))
        if item % 2 == 0 or item % 3 == 0:
            primes.append((item, "Not Prime"))
        factor = 5
        while factor * factor <= item:
```

```
        if item % factor == 0 or item % (factor + 2) == 0:
            primes.append((item, "Not Prime"))
        factor += 6
    await asyncio.sleep(1)
    return primes

async def main(data):
    odd_task = asyncio.create_task(is_odd(data))
    prime_task = asyncio.create_task(is_prime(data))
    for res in asyncio.as_completed((odd_task, prime_task)):
        compl = await res
        print(f"completed with data: {res} =>  {compl}")

asyncio.run(main([3, 5, 10, 23, 90]))
```

Here is the result:

```
completed with data: <coroutine object as_completed.._wait_for_
one at 0x10373dcc8>
=> [(3, 'Odd'), (5, 'Odd'), (10, 'Even'), (23, 'Odd'), (90,
'Even')]
completed with data: <coroutine object as_completed.._wait_for_
one at 0x10373dd48>
=> [(3, 'Prime'), (3, 'Not Prime'), (10, 'Not Prime'), (90,
'Not Prime'), (90, 'Not Prime')]
```

As you can see in the result for Listing 7-12, both tasks are running concurrently and getting the prime and odd/even numbers status based on the list passed in to both coroutines.

You can create similar tasks when using the asyncio.gather function by just using asyncio.gather instead of asyncio.as_completed, as shown in Listing 7-13.

Listing 7-13. Using asyncio.gather for Iterating on a Task

```python
import asyncio

async def is_odd(data):
    odd_even = []
    for item in data:
        odd_even.append((item, "Even") if item % 2 == 0 else
        (item, "Odd"))
    await asyncio.sleep(1)
    return odd_even

async def is_prime(data):
    primes = []
    for item in data:
        if item <= 1:
            primes.append((item, "Not Prime"))
        if item <= 3:
            primes.append((item, "Prime"))
        if item % 2 == 0 or item % 3 == 0:
            primes.append((item, "Not Prime"))
        factor = 5
        while factor * factor <= item:
            if item % factor == 0 or item % (factor + 2) == 0:
                primes.append((item, "Not Prime"))
            factor += 6
    await asyncio.sleep(1)
    return primes

async def main(data):
    odd_task = asyncio.create_task(is_odd(data))
    prime_task = asyncio.create_task(is_prime(data))
    compl = await asyncio.gather(odd_task, prime_task)
```

```
print(f"completed with data: {compl}")
return compl
```

Here is the result:

```
asyncio.run(main([3, 5, 10, 23, 90]))
completed with data:
[[(3, 'Odd'), (5, 'Odd'), (10, 'Even'), (23, 'Odd'), (90,
'Even')], [(3, 'Prime'), (3, 'Not Prime'), (10, 'Not Prime'),
(90, 'Not Prime'), (90, 'Not Prime')]]
```

You might notice that you don't need to write the loop because
asyncio.gather does that for you; it collects all the resulting data and
sends it back to the caller.

Third-Party Libraries to Consider for Async Code

Besides asyncio, there are couple of third-party libraries that can achieve
the same goals. Most of these third-party libraries try to overcome some of
the issues that you saw in asyncio.

However, considering the continuous improvements in the Python
asyncio library, I suggest using asyncio for your project unless you need
something that asyncio totally lacks.

Let's take a look at some of the third-party libraries available for
asynchronous code.

Curio

Curio is a third-party library that allows you to perform concurrent I/O
using Python coroutines. It's based on a task model that provides advanced
handling of interaction between threads and processes. Listing 7-14 shows
a simple example of writing async code using the Curio library.

Listing 7-14. Curio Example

```
import curio

async def generate(limit):
    step = 0
    while step <= limit:
        await curio.sleep(1)
        step += 1

if __name__ == "__main__":
    curio.run(generate, 10)
```

This will generate 1 to 10 numbers in an async fashion. Curio starts the kernel by calling run() and defines a task by using a method such as async def.

A task should be run inside the Curio kernel, which has the responsibility to run until there is no task to run.

Things to remember while using Curio is that it runs an async function as a task, and every task needs to be run inside the Curio kernel.

Let's look at one more example of the Curio library, which actually runs multiple tasks. See Listing 7-15.

Listing 7-15. Curio Multiple Tasks

```
import curio

async def generate(limit):
    step = 0
    while step <= limit:
        await curio.sleep(1)
        step += 1

async def say_hello():
    print("Hello")
    await curio.sleep(1000)
```

```python
async def main():
    hello_task = await curio.spawn(say_hello)
    await curio.sleep(3)

    gen_task = await curio.spawn(generate, 5)
    await gen_task.join()

    print("Welcome")
    await hello_task.join()
    print("Good by")

if __name__ == '__main__':
    curio.run(main)
```

As you might have already guessed, this shows the process of creating and joining the tasks. There are two main concepts to grasp here.

The spawn method takes a coroutine as an argument and launches the new hello_task task.

The join method waits for a task to finish before returning to the kernel.

I hope this has helped give you some idea of how Curio can achieve concurrency in Python. You can check the Curio official documentation for more details.

Trio

Trio is a modern and open source library like Curio. It promises to make it easier to write async code in Python. Some of the features that are noteworthy in Trio are the following:

- It has a good scalability mechanism.

- It can run 10,000 tasks simultaneously.

- Trio has been written in Python, which might be useful to developers who want to take a look under the hood to understand how things work.

- It is easier to get started quickly because the Trio documentation is really great. If you want to look for a specific feature, it's all documented nicely.

Let's take a quick look at a simple example of Trio to get a feel for the Trio async code. See Listing 7-16.

Listing 7-16. Trio, Simple Async Code

```python
import trio

async def greeting():
    await trio.sleep(1)
    return "Welcome to Trio!"

trio.run(greeting)

>> Welcome to Trio!
```

As you can see, it's really easy to understand what's going on with the code. Trio runs the async function using the run() method, which starts the greeting async function execution, then suspends the execution for one second, and finally returns the result.

Let's look at a little more useful example where you can run multiple tasks with Trio.

Let's convert the Listing 7-13 asyncio version of the is_odd and is_ prime async functions to Trio so you can understand better the use of Trio. See Listing 7-17.

Listing 7-17. Trio Running Multiple Tasks

```python
import trio

async def is_odd(data):
    odd_even = []
    for item in data:
        odd_even.append((item, "Even") if item % 2 == 0 else
        (item, "Odd"))
    await trio.sleep(1)
    return odd_even

async def is_prime(data):
    primes = []
    for item in data:
        if item <= 1:
            primes.append((item, "Not Prime"))
        if item <= 3:
            primes.append((item, "Prime"))
        if item % 2 == 0 or item % 3 == 0:
            primes.append((item, "Not Prime"))
        factor = 5
        while factor * factor <= item:
            if item % factor == 0 or item % (factor + 2) == 0:
                primes.append((item, "Not Prime"))
            factor += 6
    await trio.sleep(1)
    return primes

async def main(data):
    print("Calculation has started!")
    async with trio.open_nursery() as nursery:
```

```
        nursery.start_soon(is_odd, data)
        nursery.start_soon(is_prime, data)

trio.run(main, [3, 5, 10, 23, 90])
```

As you might have noticed, you haven't changed much in the is_prime and is_odd async functions because they work similarly here to asyncio.

The main difference here is the in main() function. Instead of calling asyncio.as_completed, you are using the trio.open_nursery method, which gets the nursery object. nursery starts running the async coroutines using the function nursery.start_soon.

Once nursery.start_soon wraps the async functions is_prime and is_odd, these two tasks start running in the background.

The async with statement's last block forces the main() function to stop and wait for all coroutines to finish; then it exits from nursery.

Once you run above example in Listing 7-17, you might notice that it runs like the asyncio example, where the is_prime and is_odd functions run concurrently.

Note   Curio and Trio are two notable libraries for writing async code at the time of writing this book. Having a good understanding of asyncio will help you to quickly jump on any third-party library. I suggest having a good understanding of asyncio before you opt for any third-party library because underneath most of the libraries are using some of Python async features.

Typing in Python

Python is a dynamic language, so you usually do not need worry about defining types while writing code in Python. If you are using a language like Java or .NET, you have to be aware of the types even before compiling code; otherwise, these languages will throw error.

Data types help while debugging and reading a large codebase. However, there are languages like Python and Ruby that give you the flexibility and freedom not to bother about data types and instead focus on the business logic.

Typing is one of the topics in the dynamic language world where some developers love types and some don't like to use them.

Python has types available in the form of the typing module, so I suggest giving them a try in your project to see whether they make sense for you.

I find them useful while writing code, especially while debugging and documenting the code.

Types in Python

Since Python 3, you can use types in your code. However, types are optional in Python. When you run your code, it doesn't check for types.

Even if you define the wrong types, Python won't complain about it. If you want to make sure you are writing the correct types, though, you can consider using a tool such as mypy, which complains if you don't have the right types.

Now Python allows you to add types in your code by simply adding : <data_types>. See Listing 7-18.

Listing 7-18. Adding Types in Python

```
def is_key_present(data: dict, key: str) -> bool:
    if key in data:
        return True
    else:
        return False
```

Here you are looking for a key in a dictionary by passing a dictionary and a key. The function also defines the types of parameters passed as `data: dict` and `key: str` and returns types as `-> bool`. This is mostly what you need to do to write types in Python.

Python understands this syntax and assumes you have written the right types without verifying them. However, as a developer, it gives you an idea about what types are being passed to a function.

You can use all data types natively available in Python without using any other module or library. Python supports types like `list`, `dict`, `int`, `str`, `set`, `tuple`, etc., without the need for any other module. However, there might be cases where you need more advanced types, which you will see in the next section.

typing Module

For advanced use, Python has introduced a module called `typing`, which gives you many more types to add to your codebase. It might take some initial effort to get used to the syntax and types, but once you get an understanding of the module, you might feel that it makes your code cleaner and more readable.

There is a lot of ground to cover, so let's jump straight into it. The typing module gives you the fundamental types such as `Any`, `Union`, `Tuple`, `Callable`, `TypeVar`, `Generic`, and much more. Let's briefly talk about some of these types to get idea about them.

Union

If you don't know beforehand what type will be passed to a function but the function expects to get one of the types from a limited set of types, then you can use `Union`. Here's an example:

```
from typing import Union

def find_user(user_id: Union[str, int]) -> None:
    isinstance(user_id, int):
```

```
    user_id = str(user_id)
find_user_by_id(user_id)
...
```

Here, `user_id` can be `str` or `int`, so you can use `Union` to make sure your function expects either `user_id` as `str` or `int`.

Any

This is a special kind of type; every other type is consistent with `Any`. It has all the values and all methods. You can consider using this type if you don't know which type this particular function accepts at runtime.

```
from typing import Any

def stream_data(sanitize: bool, data: Any) -> None:
    if sanitize:

        ...

    send_to_pipeline_for_processing(data)
```

Tuple

As you might guess by its name, this is a type for tuples. The only difference is that you can define the types contained by the tuple.

```
from typing import Tuple

def check_fraud_users(users_id: Tuple[int]) -> None:
    for user_id in users_id:
        try:
            check_fraud_by_id(user_id)
        exception FraudException as error:

            ...
```

TypeVar and Generics

If you want to define your own types or rename the specific types, you can utilize TypeVar from typing to do that. This is useful to make your code more readable and define types for your custom classes.

This is a more advanced concept of typing. Most of the time, you might not need it because you will find that the typing module gives you enough types to play with.

```python
from typing import TypeVar, Generics

Employee = TypeVar("Employee")
Salary = TypeVar

def get_employee_payment(emp: Generics[Employee]) -> :
    ...
```

Optional

Optional can be used when you suspect type None will also be passed as a value instead of a defined type. So, instead of writing as Union[str, None], you could simply write Optional[str].

```python
from typing import Optional

def get_user_info_by_id(user_id: Optional[int]) ->
Optional[dict]:
    if user_id:
        get_data = query_to_db_with_user_id(user_id)
        return get_data
    else:
        return None
```

This was an introduction to the typing module in Python. There are lots of other types available in the typing module that you might want to use in your existing codebase. You can refer to the Python official documentation to learn more.

```
https://docs.python.org/3/library/typing.html
```

Do Data Types Slow Code?

Using the typing module or types in general won't affect your code's performance. However, the typing module provides a method called typing.get_type_hints to return type hints for an object, which can be used by third-party tools to check for the types of an object. Python doesn't type check these at runtime, so this doesn't affect your code at all.

As per Python PEP 484[1]:

> While the proposed typing module will contain some building blocks for runtime type checking—in particular the get_type_hints() function—third party packages would have to be developed to implement specific runtime type checking functionality, for example using decorators or metaclasses. Using type hints for performance optimizations is left as an exercise for the reader.

How Typing Helps to Write Better Code

Typing can help you do static code analysis to catch type errors before you send your code to production and prevent you from some obvious bugs.

There are tools like mypy, which you can add to your toolbox as part of your software life cycle. mypy can check for correct types by running against your codebase partially or fully. mypy also helps you to detect bugs such as checking for the None type when the value is returned from a function.

Typing helps to make your code cleaner. Instead of documenting your code using comments, where you specify types in a docstring, you can use types without any performance cost.

---

[1]https://www.python.org/dev/peps/pep-0484/

If you are using an IDE like PyCharm or VSCode, the `typing` module also helps you in code completion. As you all know, early error catching and clean code are important for any large project to sustain in the long term.

Typing Pitfalls

There are some pitfalls you should be aware of while you are using the `typing` module of Python.

- **It is not well documented.** Type annotations are not well documented. It may be difficult to figure out how to write the correct types when writing custom classes or advanced data structures. This can be difficult when you are starting out with the `typing` module.

- **Types are not strict.** Because type hints are not strict, you can't guarantee a variable is of the type its annotation claims to be. In that case, you are not improving the quality of code. So, it's left up to the individual developer to write the right types. `mypy` might be a solution here to check for types.

- **There is no support for third-party libraries.** When you are using a third-party library, you might find yourself pulling your hair out as there might be lots of cases where you don't know the correct types of specific third-party tools such as with a data structure or class. You might end up using any in those cases. `mypy` also doesn't support all those third-party libraries to check for you.

> **Note**   The `typing` module certainly is a good step in the right
> direction, but there might be lot of improvement needed in the
> `typing` module. However, using `typing` right way will certainly help
> you find some subtle bugs and type errors. Using types with tools like
> mypy will certainly help to make your code cleaner.

super() Method

The `super()` method syntax now is easier to use and more readable. You
can use the `super()` method for inheritance by declaring it as follows:

```
class PaidStudent(Student):
    def __int__(self):
        super().__init__(self)
```

Type Hinting

As I mentioned, Python has a new module called `typing`, which gives you
type hints in your code.

```
import typing

def subscribed_users(limit_of_users: int) -> Dict[str, int]:
    ...
```

Better Path Handling Using pathlib

`pathlib` is a new module in Python that helps you to read files, join paths, display directory trees, and other features.

With `pathlib`, a file path can be represented by a proper `Path` object, and then you can perform a different action on that `Path` object. It has features to find the last modified file, create a unique file name, display a directory tree, count files, move and delete files, get specific components of a file, and create paths.

Let's look at an example where the `resolve()` method finds the full path of the file, as shown here:

```
import pathlib

path = pathlib.Path("error.txt")
path.resolve()
>>> PosixPath("/home/python/error.txt")

path.resolve().parent == pathlib.Path.cwd()
>>> False
```

print() Is a Function Now

`print()` is a function now. In the previous version, it was a statement.

- **Old**: `print "Sum of two numbers is", 2 + 2`

- **New**: `print("Sum of two number is", (2+2))`

f-string

Python has introduced a new and improved way to write strings, called an *f-string*. This makes the code much more readable compared to previous versions like the `%` format and `format` methods.

```
user_id = "skpl"
amount = 50
f"{user_id} has paid amount: ${amount}"
>>> skpl has paid amount: $50
```

One more reason to use an f-string is that it's faster than its previous versions.

According to PEP 498[2]:

F-strings provide a way to embed expressions inside string literals, using a minimal syntax. It should be noted that an f-string is really an expression evaluated at run time, not a constant value. In Python source code, an f-string is a literal string, prefixed with f, which contains expressions inside braces. The expressions are replaced with their values.

Keyword Only Arguments

Python now allows you to define keyword-only arguments using * as a function parameter.

```
def create_report(user, *, file_type, location):
    ...

create_report("skpl", file_type="txt", location="/user/skpl")
```

Now when you call create_report, you have to provide a keyword argument after *. You can force other developers to use positional arguments for calling the function.

---

[2]https://www.python.org/dev/peps/pep-0498/

Preserving the Order of a Dictionary

Now a dictionary preserves the order of insertion. Previously, you had to use OrderDict to do that, but now the default dictionary can do it.

```
population_raking = {}
population_raking["China"] = 1
population_raking["India"] = 2
population_raking["USA"] = 3
print(f"{population_raking}")
{'China': 1, 'India': 2, 'USA': 3}
```

Iterable Unpacking

Now Python gives you the flexibility to unpack iteratively. This is a cool feature where you can unpack variables iteratively.

```
*a, = [1]                  # a = [1]
(a, b), *c = 'PC', 5, 6    # a = "P", b = "C", c = [5, 6]
*a, = range(10)
```

Check out the official Python documentation for even more new features in Python.

Summary

This chapter focused on new major features such as asyncio and typing and minor features such as pathlib and order dictionary. However, there are plenty of other new exciting features in Python version 3.

It's always a good practice to check out the Python documentation for all the improvements. Python has great documentation that is really easy to navigate and that helps you understand any library, keyword, or module. I hope this chapter has given you enough motivation to try these features in your existing codebase or new project.

## CHAPTER 8

Debugging and Testing Python Code

If you are writing code, especially for production, it's really important that the code has good logging features and test cases. Both make sure that you can track errors and fix any issues that arise. Python has a rich set of built-in libraries for debugging and testing the Python code that I'll cover in this chapter.

Note   As with any programming language, Python has a lot of tools to add logs and tests in code. Having a good understanding of those tools is important in a professional environment where running software in production makes money for you. Losing money because of errors or bugs in your production code can be disastrous for a company or product. Therefore, you need to have logging and testing in place before you push your code to production. It also helps to have some kind of metric and performance tracking tool so you can get an idea of how things will be when your software is used in the real world by hopefully millions of users.

© Sunil Kapil 2019
S. Kapil, *Clean Python*, https://doi.org/10.1007/978-1-4842-4878-2_8

Debugging

Debugging is one of the most important skills to have as a developer. Most developers don't put in enough effort to learn debugging; they usually just try different things when it's needed. Debugging should not be an afterthought process; it's a technique to rule out different hypotheses before coming to any conclusion about an actual issue in the code. In this section, you will explore techniques and tools to debug your Python code.

Debugging Tools

In this section, I will go over `pdb`, `ipdb`, and `pudb`.

pdb

`pdb` is one of the most useful command-line tools for debugging Python code. `pdb` provides stack information and parameter information and jumps around the code commands inside the `pdb` debugger. To set up the debugger in the Python code, you can write something like this:

```
import pdb
pdb.set_trace()
```

Once control hits the line where the `pdb` debugger is enabled, you can debug your code using the `pdb` command-line options. `pdb` gives you the following commands:

- h: Help command
- w: Prints the stack trace
- d: Moves the current frame count down
- u: Moves the current frame count up
- s: Executes the current line

- n: Continues execution until the next line

- unt [line number]: Continues execution until a line number

- r: Continues execution until the current function returns

There are other command-line options in pdb. You can check out all of them at https://docs.python.org/3/library/pdb.html.

ipdb

Similar to pdb, ipdb is a debugger command-line tool. It gives you the same power as pdb with the added advantage that you can use ipdb on IPython. You can add the ipdb debugger as follows:

```
import ipdb
ipdb.set_trace()
```

Once it's installed, you can check all the available commands in ipdb. Mostly, these are similar to pdb, as follows:

```
ipdb> ?

Documented commands (type help <topic>):
==========================================
EOF     bt        cont      enable  jump  pdef    psource  run      unt
a       c         continue  exit    l     pdoc    q        s        until
alias   cl        d         h       list  pfile   quit     step     up
args    clear     debug     help    n     pinfo   r        tbreak   w
b       commands  disable   ignore  next  pinfo2  restart  u        whatis
break   condition down      j       p     pp      return   unalias  where
```

```
Miscellaneous help topics:
==========================
exec   pdb

Undocumented commands:
======================
retval   rv
```

You can find more information about ipdb at https://pypi.org/project/ipdb/.

ipdb has the same command-line options as pdb, as shown here:

- h: Help command

- w: Prints the stack trace

- d: Moves the current frame count down

- u: Moves the current frame count up

- s: Executes the current line

- n: Continues execution until the next line

- unt [line number]: Continues execution until a line number

- r: Continues execution until the current function returns

pudb

pudb is little feature-rich debugging tool that has more features than pdb and ipdb. It's a visual debugger based in the console. You can debug the code when you are writing it instead of jumping to a command line like with pdb or ipdb. It more looks like a GUI debugger but runs on the console, which makes it lightweight compared to GUI debuggers.

You can add the debugger in code by adding the following line:

```
import pudb
pudb.set_trace()
```

It has good documentation. You can find out more information about pudb and all of its features at https://documen.tician.de/pudb/starting.html.

You can use the following keys when you are in the pudb debugging interface:

- n: Executes the next command

- s: Steps into a function

- c: Continues execution

- b: Sets a breakpoint on the current line

- e: Shows the traceback from a thrown exception

- q: Opens a dialog to either quit or restart the running program

- o: Shows the original console/standard output screen

- m: Opens a module in a different file

- L: Goes to a line

- !: Goes to the Python command-line subwindow at the bottom of the screen

- ?: Displays the help dialog that includes a complete listing of shortcut commands

- <SHIFT+V>: Switches the context to the variable subwindow on the right of the screen

- <SHIFT+B>: Switches the context to the breakpoints subwindow on the right of the screen

- <CTRL+X>: Toggles contexts between the lines of code and the Python command line

As an example, once you are in the pudb display, pressing b will set a breakpoint on that line where execution stops after continuing with the c shortcut. One useful option is to set up a variable condition under which the breakpoint applies. Once the condition is satisfied, control will stop at that point.

You can also configure pudb by creating a file like ~/.config/pudb/ pudb.cfg, as given here:

```
[pudb]
breakpoints_weight = 0.5
current_stack_frame = top
custom_stringifier =
custom_theme =
display = auto
line_numbers = True
prompt_on_quit = True
seen_welcome = e027
shell = internal
sidebar_width = 0.75
stack_weight = 0.5
stringifier = str
theme = classic
variables_weight = 1.5
wrap_variables = True
```

breakpoint

breakpoint is a new keyword introduced in Python 3.7. It gives you the capability to debug the code. breakpoint is similar to the other command-line tools discussed. You can write the code as follows:

```
x = 10
breakpoint()
y = 20
```

breakpoint also can be configured using the PYTHONBREAKPOINT environment variable to provide the debugger with a method to be called by the breakpoint() function. This is helpful because you can change the debugger module easily without making any code changes. As an example, if you want to disable debugging, you can use PYTHONBREAKPOINT=0.

Use the Logging Module Instead of print in Production Code

As mentioned, logging is an important part of any software product, and Python has a library called logging. Logging also helps you understand the flow of the code. If you have logging available, it gives you an idea of where things are failing by providing a stack trace. You can use the logging library simply by importing the library as follows:

```
import logging
logging.getLogger(__name__).addHandler(logging.NullHandler())
```

The logging library has five standard levels that indicate the severity of events. See Table 8-1.

Table 8-1. *Logging Standard Levels*

Level	Numeric Value
CRITICAL	50
ERROR	40
WARNING	30
INFO	20
DEBUG	10
NOTSET	0

So, you can write something like Listing 8-1.

Listing 8-1. Logging Configuration

```python
import logging
from logging.config import dictConfig

logging_config = dict(
    version=1,
    formatters={
        'f': {'format':
                  '%(asctime)s %(name)-12s %(levelname)-8s
                  %(message)s'}
    },
    handlers={
        'h': {'class': 'logging.StreamHandler',
              'formatter': 'f',
              'level': logging.DEBUG}
    },
```

```
    root={
        'handlers': ['h'],
        'level': logging.DEBUG,
    },
)
```

```
dictConfig(logging_config)
```

```
logger = logging.getLogger()
logger.debug("This is debug logging")
```

Let's say you want to capture the whole stack trace of the log; you can do something like Listing 8-2.

Listing 8-2. Stack Trace Logging

```
import logging

a = 90
b = 0

try:
  c = a / b
except Exception as e:
  logging.error("Exception ", exc_info=True)
```

Classes and Functions in Logging

The logging module has a number of classes and functions that can be used to define your own logging class and configure logging for your specific needs and project.

The most commonly used classes defined in the logging module are the following:

- Logger: This is part of the logging module and is called by the application directly to get the logger object. It has a number of methods, listed here:

  - setLevel: This sets the level of logging. When the logger is created, it is set to NOSET.

  - isEnableFor: This method checks the logging level set by logging.disable(level).

  - debug: This logs the message with level DEBUG on this logger.

  - info: This logs the message with INFO on this logger.

  - warning: This logs the message with WARNING on this logger.

  - error: This logs the message with level ERROR on this logger.

  - critical: This logs a message with level CRITICAL on this logger.

  - log: This logs the message with an integer level on this logger.

  - exception: This logs a message with level ERROR on this logger.

  - addHandler: This adds the specified handler to this logger.

- Handler: Handler is a base class of other useful handler classes such as StreamHandler, FileHandler, SMTPHandler, HTTPHandler, and more. These subclasses send the logging outputs to the corresponding destinations, like sys.stdout or a disk file.

- createLock: This initializes the thread lock that can be used to serialize access to underlying I/O functionality.

- setLevel: This sets the handler to a level.

- flush: This ensures that the logging output has been flushed.

- close: Subclasses of Handler ensure that this gets called from the overridden close() method.

- format: This does the formatting for the output logging.

- emit: Actually, this logs the specified logging message.

- Formatter: This is where you specify the format of the output by specifying a string format that lists the attributes that the output should contain.

  - format: This formats the string.

  - formatTime: This formats the time. It's used with time.strftime() to format the creation time of the record. The default is '%Y-%m-%d %H:%M:%S, uuu', where uuu is in milliseconds.

  - formatException: This formats the specific exception information.

  - formatStack: This formats stack information on the string.

You can also configure logging for a running application, as shown in Listing 8-3.

Listing 8-3. Logging Configuration File

```
[loggers]
keys=root,sampleLogger

[handlers]
keys=consoleHandler

[formatters]
keys=sampleFormatter

[logger_root]
level=DEBUG
handlers=consoleHandler

[logger_sampleLogger]
level=DEBUG
handlers=consoleHandler
qualname=sampleLogger
propagate=0

[handler_consoleHandler]
class=StreamHandler
level=DEBUG
formatter=sampleFormatter
args=(sys.stdout,)

[formatter_sampleFormatter]
format=%(asctime)s - %(name)s - %(levelname)s - %(message)s
```

Now you can use this config file, as shown in Listing 8-4.

Listing 8-4. Use Logging Configuration

```python
import logging
import logging.config

logging.config.fileConfig(fname='logging.conf', disable_
existing_loggers=False)

# Get the logger specified in the file
logger = logging.getLogger(__name__)

logger.debug('Debug logging message')
```

This is the same configuration as the YAML file shown in Listing 8-5.

Listing 8-5. Logging Configuration in YAML

```yaml
version: 1
formatters:
  simple:
    format: '%(asctime)s - %(name)s - %(levelname)s - %(message)s'
handlers:
  console:
    class: logging.StreamHandler
    level: DEBUG
    formatter: simple
    stream: ext://sys.stdout
loggers:
  sampleLogger:
    level: DEBUG
    handlers: [console]
    propagate: no
root:
  level: DEBUG
  handlers: [console]
```

You can read this file as shown in Listing 8-6.

Listing 8-6. Use Logging Configuration YAML File

```python
import logging
import logging.config
import yaml

with open('logging.yaml', 'r') as f:
    config = yaml.safe_load(f.read())
    logging.config.dictConfig(config)

logger = logging.getLogger(__name__)

logger.debug('Debug logging message')
```

You can find more information about logging at `https://docs.python.org/3/library/logging.html`.

Use the metrics Library for Identifying Bottlenecks

I have seen lot of developers who don't understand the value of metrics in production code. Metrics collect different data points from code, such as the number of errors in a specific part of code or the response time of a third-party API. Metrics also can be defined to capture specific data points such as the number of users currently logged in to a web application. Metrics are usually collected per request, per second, per minute, or on a regular interval to monitor a system over time.

There are a lot of third-party applications for collection metrics on production code such as New Relic, Datadog, and so on. There are different kinds of metrics that you can collect. You can categorize them as performance metrics or resource metrics. Performance metrics could be as follows:

- **Throughput**: This is the amount of work the system is doing per unit time.

- **Error**: This is the number of error results or rate of errors per unit time.

- **Performance**: This represents the time required to complete a unit of work.

Besides these points, there are several data points that you can use to capture the performance of your application. Other than performance metrics, there are metrics like resource metrics that you can use to get resource metrics like this:

- **Utilization**: This is the percent of time a resource is busy.

- **Availability**: This is the time that a resource responded to a request.

Before using metrics, consider which kind of data point you want to use to track your application. Using metrics will definitely make you more confident about your application, and you can measure your application performance.

How IPython Is Helpful

IPython is a REPL tool for Python. IPython helps you to run your code at the command line and test it without much configuration. IPython is a really intelligent and mature REPL; it has a lot of features like tab completion and magic functions like %timeit, %run, and so on. You can also get the history and debug your code inside IPython. There are some debugging tools that explicitly work on IPython like `ipdb`.

The main features of IPython are as follows:

- Comprehensive object introspection

- Input history, which is persistent across sessions

- Caching of output results during a session with automatically generated references

- Extensible tab completion, with support by default for completion of Python variables and keywords, file names, and function keywords

- Extensible system of "magic" commands for controlling the environment and performing many tasks related to IPython or the operating system

- A rich configuration system with easy switching between different setups (simpler than changing the `$PYTHONSTARTUP` environment variable every time)

- Session logging and reloading

- Extensible syntax processing for special-purpose situations

- Access to the system shell with a user-extensible alias system

- Easily embeddable in other Python programs and GUIs

- Integrated access to the `pdb` debugger and the Python profiler

The command-line interface inherits the previously listed functionality and adds the following:

- Real multiline editing thanks to `prompt_toolkit`

- Syntax highlighting as you type

- Integration with a command-line editor for a better workflow

When used with a compatible front end, the kernel allows the following:

- Objects that can create a rich display of HTML, images, LaTEX, sound, and video

- Interactive widgets with the use of the `ipywidgets` package

You can install IPython as follows:

```
pip install ipython
```

Getting started with IPython is really easy; you can just type the command `ipython`, and you will be in the `ipython` command shell, as shown here:

`Python 3.7.0`

Type 'copyright', 'credits' or 'license' for more information

IPython 6.4.0 -- An enhanced Interactive Python. Type '?' for help.

In [1]:

Now you can start using the `ipython` command like this:

```
In [1]: print("hello ipython")
```

You can find more information about IPython at `https://ipython.readthedocs.io/en/stable/interactive/index.html`.

Testing

For any software application, having test code is as important as having application code. Testing makes sure you are not deploying buggy code. Python has a lot of useful libraries that make it easier to write different kinds of tests.

Why Testing Is Important

Testing is as important as your actual code. Testing makes sure that the shipping code works as expected. You should start writing testing code as soon as you start writing the first line of your application code. Testing should not be an afterthought and should not be there just for the sake of testing. Testing should make sure that every piece of code results in the expected behavior.

There are a couple of reasons you should consider writing tests as early as possible in your software development life cycle.

- To make sure that you are build the right thing, it's important to have tests in your software life cycle as soon as you start writing code. It's hard to make sure that you are in the right path if you don't have tests to check expected behavior.

- You want early detection of any breaking changes. When you are making changes in one part of the code, there is a high probability that it will break some other part of the code. You want to detect that breaking code early instead of after going to production.

- Testing also plays a role in documenting your code. Tests are a really useful way to document your code without specifically writing documentation for every part of the code.

- Another advantage of having tests is for onboarding new developers. When a new developer joins the team, they can start getting familiar with the code by running and reading the tests, which can give you an idea of the flow of the code.

If you want to make sure that your code works as you expect and your users have a good time using the software, you should use tests in your production code.

Pytest vs. UnitTest

Python has lot of amazing testing libraries. Pytest and UnitTest are two of the most famous libraries. In this section, you will look at the main differences between these two libraries so you can decide which one you want to use to test your code.

Both are popular libraries; however, there are multiple differences between them that make people choose one over another. Let's look some of the main features you want to consider before deciding which one to choose.

Pytest is a third-party library, and UnitTest is a built-in library in Python. To use Pytest, you have to install it, but this is not a big deal.

```
pip install pytest
```

UnitTest needs to inherit `TestCase` and needs to have a class to write and run tests. Pytest is more flexible in this regard, as you can write tests by function or by class. Listing 8-7 shows UnitTest, while Listing 8-8 shows Pytest.

Listing 8-7. UnitTest Example 1

```python
from unittest import TestCase

class SimpleTest(TestCase):
    def test_simple(self):
        self.assertTrue(True)

    def test_tuple(self):
        self.assertEqual((1, 3, 4), (1, 3, 4))

    def test_str(self):
        self.assertEqual('This is unit test', 'this is')
```

Listing 8-8. Pytest Example 1

```python
import pytest

def test_simple():
    assert 2 == 2

def test_tuple():
    assert (1, 3, 4) == (1, 3, 4)
```

As you might have noticed, UnitTest uses the `TestCase` instance method; however, Pytest has a built-in assert. Pytest asserts are easier to read without knowing about different assert methods. However, UnitTest assertions are more configurable and have more methods to assert.

You can see all the assert methods of UnitTest at `https://docs. python.org/3/library/unittest.html#assert-methods` and of Pytest at `https://docs.pytest.org/en/latest/reference.html`.

Listing 8-9 shows UnitTest, and Listing 8-10 shows Pytest.

Listing 8-9. UnitTest Example 2

```python
from unittest import TestCase

class SimpleTest(TestCase):
    def not_equal(self):
        self.assertNotEqual(2, 3)  # 2 != 3

    def assert_false(self):
        x = 0
        self.assertFalse(x)   # bool(x) is false

    def assert_in(self):
        self.assertIn(5, [1, 3, 8, 5])    # 5 in [1, 3, 8, 5]
```

Listing 8-10. Pytest Example 2

```python
import pytest

def not_equal():
    assert 2 != 2

def assert_false():
    x = 0
    assert x is 0

def assert_in():
    assert 5 in [1, 3, 8, 5]
```

You might notice that Pytest is easier to assert compared to UnitTest. Pytest is also more readable compared to UnitTest.

Pytest highlights errors with code snippets, while UnitTest doesn't have that feature; it shows a one-line error with no highlights. This might change in future versions, but currently Pytest has better error reporting. Listing 8-11 shows the Pytest console output, while Listing 8-12 shows the UnitTest console output.

Listing 8-11. Pytest Console Output

```
>>> py.test simple.py
============================== test session starts =============
platform darwin -- Python 3.7.0 -- py-1.4.20 -- pytest-2.5.2
plugins: cache, cov, pep8, xdist
collected 2 items

simple.py .F


==================================== FAILURES =================
_____ test_simple_____

    def test_simple():
        print("This test should fail")
>       assert False
E       assert False

simple.py:7: AssertionError
-------------------------------- Captured stdout ---------------
This test should fail
======================= 1 failed, 1 passed in 0.04 seconds ====
```

Listing 8-12. UnitTest Console Output

```
Traceback (most recent call last):
  File "~<stdin>~", line 11, in simple.py
ZeroDivisionError: integer division or modulo by zero
```

Pytest has setup methods like `fixture` that you can configure for modules, sessions, and functions. UnitTest has the methods `setUp` and `tearDown`. Listing 8-13 shows the Pytest fixture, while Listing 8-14 shows the UnitTest fixture.

Listing 8-13. Pytest Fixture

```python
import pytest

@pytest.fixture
def get_instance():
    s = CallClassBeforeStartingTest()
    s.call_function()
    return s

@pytest.fixture(scope='session')
def test_data():
    return {"test_data": "This is test data which will be use
    in different test methods"}

def test_simple(test_data, get_instance):
    assert test_instance.call_another_function(test_data) is
    not None
```

Listing 8-14. UnitTest Tests Using Setup and Teardown

```python
from unittest import TestCase

class SetupBaseTestCase(TestCase):
    def setUp(self):
        self.sess = CallClassBeforeStartingTest()

    def test_simple():
        self.sess.call_function()

    def tearDown(self):
        self.sess.close()
```

As you will notice, Pytest and UnitTest have different ways of handling the test setup. These are some of the main differences between Pytest and UnitTest. However, both are feature-rich tools.

I usually prefer to use Pytest because it is easy to use and readable. However, if you are comfortable using UnitTest, please don't feel you have to use Pytest. Use whatever you are comfortable with. Choosing a testing tool is secondary; the primary goal should be having good tests for your code!

Property Testing

Property testing is way to test functions where you provide numbers of input. You can read more about it at `https://hypothesis.works/articles/what-is-property-based-testing/`.

Python has a library called `hypothesis` that is perfect for writing property testing. `hypothesis` is easy to use, and if you are familiar with Pytest, it is even easier.

You can install `hypothesis` as follows:

```
pip install hypothesis
```

You can see an example of property testing using `hypothesis`, as shown in Listing 8-15.

Listing 8-15. Property Testing

```
from hypothesis import given
from hypothesis.strategies import text

@given(text())
def test_decode_inverts_encode(s):
    assert decode(encode(s)) == s
```

Here, `hypothesis` provides all kinds of text to test the function `test_decode_inverts_encode` instead of you providing that set of data to decode the text.

How to Create a Report for Testing

There are lots of tools that will generate a test report. In fact, Pytest and UnitTest will do this. Test reports help to understand the test results and are useful to track the progress of test coverage as well. However, here I am strictly talking about the test report generation.

When you run a test, report generation can give you the full overview of running a test with the pass/fail results. You can use one of the following tools to do this:

```
pip install pytest-html
pytest -v tests.py --html=pytest_report.html --self-contained-html
```

One tool called nose has built-in report generation tools. If you are using nose, you can generate tests by running the command as follows:

```
nosetests -with-coverage --cover-html
```

With UnitTest, you can use TextTestRunner, as shown in Listing 8-16.

Listing 8-16. UnitTest with TextTestRunner Part 1

```python
class TestBasic(unittest.TestCase):
    def setUp(self):
        # set up in here

class TestA(TestBasic):
    def first_test(self):
        self.assertEqual(10,10)

    def second_test(self):
        self.assertEqual(10,5)
```

245

Let's assume you have the previous test to run. UnitTest provides you with a method called TextTestRunner to generate the report for the test, as shown in Listing 8-17.

Listing 8-17. UnitTest with TextTestRunner Part 2

```
import test

test_suite = unittest.TestLoader().loadTestFromModule(test)
test_results = unittest.TextTestRunner(verbosity=2).run(test_
suite)
```

If you run this code, it will generate the report for the TestBasic class.

Besides the tools discussed here, there are plenty of Python third-party libraries that provide a lot of flexibility in terms of the way to generate reports, and they are very powerful tools.

Automate Unit Tests

Automating unit tests means that unit tests run without you having to start them. Having the capability to run a unit test while merging with the master or main code means you can make sure that new changes don't break any existing feature or functionality.

As I have already discussed, having unit tests for any codebase is really important, and you'll want to run them using some kind of CI/CD flow. This also assumes that you are using some kind of version control like Git or third-party tools like GitHub or GitLab to store your code.

The ideal flow to run tests is as follows:

1.   Commit changes using version control.

2.   Push the changes to some kind of version control.

3. Trigger the unit tests from version control using some third-party tool like Travis, which runs the tests automatically and posts the results to version control.

4. Version control should not allow merging to the master until a test passes.

Getting Your Code Ready for Production

Before going to production, there are things that are important to make sure that shipped code is high-quality and works as expected. Every team or company has different steps they take before deploying changes or new code to production. I won't discuss any one ideal process to deploy to production. However, you can introduce some things in your current deployment pipeline to make your Python code better and less error prone in production.

Run Unit and Integration Tests in Python

As already mentioned, it's important to have unit tests. Besides unit tests, having integration tests helps immensely, especially if you have a lot of moving part in the codebase.

As you know, unit tests help to check a specific unit of the code and make sure that unit of code works. With integration tests, it's important to test if one part of the code works with another part of the code without any error. Integration tests help you to check that the code works as a whole.

Use Linting to Make Code Consistent

A code linter analyzes your source code for potential errors. Linters solve the following issues in your code:

- Syntax errors

- Structural problems like the use of undefined variables

- Code style guideline violations

Code linting gives you information that can be easily skimmed. It's really useful for code especially for a big project when there is a lot of moving code and all the developers who are working on code can agree on a specific code style.

There is a lot of Python linting code. Which type you should use is up to you or your team of developers.

There are a lot of advantages to using linting.

- It helps you write better code by checking it against coding standards.

- It prevents you from making obvious bugs such as syntax errors, typos, bad formatting, incorrect styling, and so on.

- It saves your time as a developer.

- It helps all developers agree on specific code standards.

- It's really easy to use and configure.

- It's easy to set up.

Let's look at some of the popular linting tools available in Python. If you are using a modern IDE tool like VSCode, Sublime, or PyCharm, you will find that these tools already have some kind of linting available.

flake8

flake8 is one of the most popular linting tools. It's a wrapper of pep8, pyflakes, and circular complexity. It has a low rate of false positives.

You can easily set it up by using this command:

```
pip install flake8
```

pylint

pylint is another great choice for linting. It needs a bit more setup and gives more false positives compared to flake8, but if you need more rigorous linting checks on your code, pylint might be right tool for you.

Use Code Coverage to Check for Tests

Code coverage is a process where you check for a number of tests written for code (or the code that is touched by different tests to be precise). Code coverage makes sure you have enough tests to be sure about the quality of the code. Code coverage should be one part of your software development life cycle; it continuously raises the quality standard of your code.

Python has tool called Coverage.py, which is a third-party tool to check for test coverage. You can install it as follows:

```
pip install coverage
```

On installation of Coverage.py, a Python script called coverage is placed in your Python script directory. Coverage.py has a number of commands that determine the action performed.

- run: Runs a Python program and collects execution data

- report: Reports coverage results

- html: Produces annotated HTML listings with coverage results

- xml: Produces an XML report with coverage results

- annotate: Annotates source files with coverage results

- erase: Erases previously collected coverage data

- combine: Combines a number of data files

- debug: Gets diagnostic information

You can run a coverage report as follows:

```
coverage run -m packagename.modulename arg1 arg2
```

There are other tools that are directly integrated with version control systems like GitHub. These tools can be more convenient for bigger teams because the checks can be run as soon as new code is submitted for review. Having code coverage as part of the software life cycle makes sure you are not taking any chances with your production code.

Use virtualenv for Your Project

virtualenv is one of the tools that should be part of every developer's toolchain. You use it to create isolated Python environments. When you install virtualenv and create an environment for your project, virtualenv creates a folder that contains all the executables that your project needs to run.

You can install virtualenv as follows:

```
pip install virtualenv
```

I suggest looking here to get more information about virtualenv:

```
https://docs.python-guide.org/dev/virtualenvs/
```

Summary

For any production code, it's important to have tools that help you to debug and better monitor your code. As you learned in this chapter, Python has plenty of tools that give you the capability to better prepare your code before you deploy it to production. These tools not only help you stay sane when your application is used by millions of users but also help you maintain your code for long-term use. Make sure you are leveraging these tools for your application as investing in these tools will definitely pay off in the long run. Having the right process when deploying your application in production is as important as building new features because it will make sure that your application is high-quality.

APPENDIX

Some Awesome Python Tools

This appendix lists some recommended tools that will help speed up your development and improve your code quality. You might be using them already, but if not, I suggest making them part of your code base as these tools can help developers spot bugs early on and improve code maintenance.

Sphinx

Just like writing unit tests is important to maintaining code quality, having well-documented code is important to making sure that new developers who join the project can ramp up quickly without getting lost in the code. Sphinx can help you document your code easily. You just need to make sure to add a docstring in your code.

You can install Sphinx as follows:

```
pip install sphinx
```

Next, create a docs folder in your project as follows:

```
project
    project_name
        __init__.py
        source_1.py
        source_2.py
```

© Sunil Kapil 2019
S. Kapil, *Clean Python*, https://doi.org/10.1007/978-1-4842-4878-2

```
docs
setup.py
```

From within your docs folder, when you run the sphinx-quickstart script, the script can perform the necessary setup. This is how you run the command:

```
cd docs
sphinx-quickstart
```

This script creates a number of directories and files within the docs folder, which will be used to autogenerate documentation from your source code.

Now you can add a docstring in your code as follows:

```
"""

Module perform some basic claculation tasks.

"""


class Calculation:
    """This class performs different calculations.

    You can use this class to do various calculations which
    make sure that you get the right results.
    """

    def __init__(self):
        """Calculation initialization method."""
        self.current_number = 0

    def sum(self, list_of_numbers):
        """Add provide list of numbers and return sum.

        param list_of_numbers: list of numbers need to added.
        type list_of_numners: list
        return: return sum of numbers.
```

```
type: int
"""

return sum(list_of_numbers)
```

Now if you want to generate an HTML file, you can use the following command:

```
make html
```

This will generate an HTML file as your documentation, based on comments you added in the code.

Coverage

Coverage helps you to measure the code coverage of your Python code. Its main purpose is to gauge the effectiveness of tests. It shows you which part of the code is being tested and generates a report based on your tests. It supports most major Python versions.

Coverage looks for a `.coverage` file in your project to read and use to generate a report for you. You can install Coverage by running the following command:

```
pip install pytest-cov
```

If you are using `pytest`, then you can run it as follows:

```
py.test test.py --cov=sample.py
```

You will need the `py.test` plug-in for `pytest` to generate a report using Coverage. It displays the report as follows:

```
Name | Stmts | Miss | Cover | Missing |
.......................................
sample.py | 6 | 0 | 100% |
```

You can find more information about Coverage at `https://coverage.readthedocs.io/en/latest/index.html`.

pre-commit

If you are using the Git version control system to manage your project, then a pre-commit hook is one of the tools that should be part of your commit process. pre-commit hooks are Git hook scripts that run when you try to commit the code; this helps you to identify various issues before your submission for code review.

Issues that might be identified include missing semicolons, typos, code structure issues, poor coding style, complexity, trailing whitespaces, debug statements, and so on.

By pointing out these issues, you can fix them before submitting for code review and save the reviewer and the rest of the team time and effort.

You can hook up your linter such as Flake8 or Pylint with pre-commit to identify all these issues before you submit your code. You can install the pre-commit package manager as follows:

```
pip install pre-commit
```

To add the pre-commit hook, you can create a file as follows:

```
pre-commit-config.yaml
```

In this file you can define all the hooks that you want to run before submitting code.

When you try to commit any code with issues, it errors out all those issues and won't allow you to commit before fixing them. This also ensures that all team members are following a similar style and checking their code against tools like flak8 or pylint.

You can also create your own new hooks and add them as part of the code submission process. You can learn more about pre-commit here: https://pre-commit.com/.

Pyenv for virtualenv

Pyenv helps you manage different versions of Python with different virtual environments. You can work with Python versions such as python2.7, python3.7, python3.8, etc., at the same time on one machine and switch between them easily. It also can switch your virtual env for you by changing the directory.

You can install Pyenv by going to https://github.com/pyenv/pyenv-installer.

Once, you install Pyenv, you can set these lines in your .bashrc file:

```
export PATH="~/.pyenv/bin:$PATH"
eval "$(pyenv init -)"
eval "$(pyenv virtualenv-init -)"
```

Now you can explore different Pyenv commands by reading the documentation at https://github.com/pyenv/pyenv

Jupyter Lab

If you work in the data science field, you might have heard about using Jupyter or Notebook to run the code in a browser. There is a new tool available that is an improved version of Notebook and Jupyter called Jupyter Lab.

You can also consider it as an IDE for Python; it can run all kinds of Python code. It's recommended for data science people because they don't need to set up several Python virtual environments or debug virtual environment issues. Using Jupyter Lab saves you from all those environment issues, and you can focus on writing your code.

You can use pip to install Jupyter Lab for you, as shown here:

```
python3 -m pip install jupyterlab
```

Or you can use conda, as shown here:

```
conda install -c conda-forge jupyterlab
```

To run it, you can simply write jupyter lab.

This will open your default browser to http://localhost:8888/lab, where you can start writing your Python code.

Pycharm/VSCode/Sublime

There are some great IDEs that help you to write your Python code such as Pycharm by JetBrains, VSCode by Microsoft, or Sublime. These are some of the notable IDEs that are popular among the developers.

Pycharm comes in community and license versions. VSCode and Sublime are open source code, and you can use them for free.

All of these are great tools for programming, so it's a matter of preference which one you choose. They give you out-of-the-box features such as IntelliSense, remote debugging, and much more.

Flake8/Pylint

Like every other language, Python has some guidelines to write the code in a Pythonic way. Tools like Flake8 and Pylint make sure that you are following all the Python guidelines. These tools are configurable, so you can modify the checks per your project needs.

You can install Pylint in your virtual environment by pip as follows:

```
pip install pylint
```

As mentioned, Pylint is totally configurable. You can use a file like pylintrc to customize which errors or conventions are important to you. You can also write your own plug-in to customize it.

Similarly, Flake8 checks for all PEP8 rules in your code and tells you if you are breaking any.

You can install Flake8 as follows:

```
pip install flake8
```

Flake8 also has a configuration file called `.flake8` to customize checks for you per your needs.

You don't need to install both of them as they are tools to achieve the same goal, which is to make your code follow the PEP8 rules.

Index

Printed in the United States
By Bookmasters